PROOF OF
GOD

A Conversation between
Doubt and Reason

Douglas Ell

ISBN 978-1-64468-239-5 (Paperback)
ISBN 978-1-64468-240-1 (Digital)

Covenant Books, Inc.
11661 Hwy 707
Murrells Inlet, SC 29576
www.covenantbooks.com

Doubt and Reason are familiar to all. Here they discuss the existence of God. We give Doubt a powerful dose of skepticism, and Reason knowledge of all current science.

The Numbers Proof

DOUBT. How do you prove the existence of God?

REASON. Evidence! Facts! Things with *no other explanation*! You know what they say—"When you have eliminated the impossible, whatever remains, however improbable, must be the truth."

"WHEN YOU HAVE ELIMINATED THE IMPOSSIBLE, WHATEVER REMAINS, HOWEVER IMPROBABLE, MUST BE THE TRUTH."

- SHERLOCK HOLMES

DOUBT. They? What bozo said that?

REASON. Sherlock Holmes.

DOUBT. Who's he?

REASON. I like a literary person.

DOUBT. Whatever. No such evidence.

REASON. There is! Undeniable! To me, and to many, science now proves God.

DOUBT. You can't prove God!

If there are things for which God is the *only* explanation, then God is real.

REASON. I can prove God three ways.

DOUBT. Banana peels. Give me a hint.

REASON. Every kind of animal has working code that is new and doesn't resemble the code in any other kind of animal. You—

DOUBT. Back up. What's *code?*

REASON. Instructions for doing something.

DOUBT. Like computer code?

REASON. Yes, or writing, or other systems for transferring information. Code can be letters, numbers, symbols, or even objects. Life uses groups of atoms.

DOUBT. Atoms? Cool. But so what? Just because different animals have different code, that doesn't prove anything.

REASON. It does. You can't get new, unrelated, unique working codes by chance. The codes couldn't have *evolved* by accident. They were designed, by God.

DOUBT. Supposing, just pretend imagine fantasy supposing that were true, what would it prove?

REASON. There is a God. Every kind of animal was designed.

DOUBT. No way! Like you're telling me each was designed? Like some super transcendent intelligence designed every creature on Earth? Ha!

REASON. That is *exactly* what I am saying.

DOUBT. Why would I believe that?

REASON. Because science—observation, experimentation, and reasoning—proves it's true. There is *no other explanation*. New working code in different kinds of animals—code that doesn't resemble any other working code—is positive evidence of God. You can't—

DOUBT. Don't believe you.

REASON. Doesn't matter what you *believe!* Here's another quote. "The great thing about science is it's true whether or not you believe in it."

DOUBT. Who said that?

REASON. Neil deGrasse Tyson.

DOUBT. The guy on the Cosmos series?

REASON. Yes.

DOUBT. He's an atheist! He said that to smack religion!

REASON. He did, but it destroys his atheism. The facts *prove* design, and it doesn't matter whether you *believe* in God. Science *proves* there is a God. There is *no other explanation*.

DOUBT. You can prove God three ways?

REASON. Yes! I heard you like numbers, so let's start with the numbers proof. It's not hard. No formulas. I will use numbers to prove the code used to build every kind of animal was designed by God.

DOUBT. You're crazy. And don't try to sneak anything by me. You just made three claims, not one. You need to prove *each*. First is all life runs code. Second is you can't really get new working code by chance. Third is every kind of animal has working code that is new and unique, that doesn't resemble the code in any other kind of animal. You need to prove *all three*.

1. ALL LIFE RUNS CODE.

2. YOU CAN'T REALLY GET NEW WORKING CODE BY CHANCE.

3. EVERY KIND OF ANIMAL HAS WORKING CODE THAT IS NEW AND UNIQUE, THAT DOESN'T RESEMBLE THE CODE IN ANY OTHER KIND OF ANIMAL.

REASON. Brilliant.

DOUBT. Did I get that right?

REASON. Brilliant. Couldn't have said it better myself. Absolutely brilliant. I am in the presence of a genius.

DOUBT. People say I'm like Einstein.

REASON. Could be your hair.

Step 1: All Life Runs Code

DOUBT. Your first claim is stupid. Computers run code, not life.

REASON. Ever hear of deoxyribonucleic acid?

DOUBT. D-what?

REASON. DNA. It's a code with four *letters*; four special groups of atoms.

DOUBT. Of course. DNA is code?

REASON. Yes. That shocked people. It is *the* most important discovery in biology in the last century. In 1953, scientists discovered that the information of life is stored in a four-*letter* DNA code. The *letters* that make up the code are special groups of atoms.

DOUBT. Computers use a binary code, don't they? Just two possibilities at each spot, not four?

REASON. You are smart. Yes, in some computer code, there are two possible items at each position. In DNA, there are four. I like this quote—"DNA is biological computer code, only far, far more advanced than anything we have ever built."

> **DNA is biological computer code, only far, far more advanced than anything we have ever built.**
> **—Bill Gates**

DOUBT. You and your quotes. Who said that?

REASON. Bill Gates.

DOUBT. That Microsoft guy, who made a fortune writing code, writing instructions for computers? You think he knows code?

REASON. Maybe.

DOUBT. Okay. So DNA uses a code of four *letters*, and computers use a code of two *letters*. Any other examples?

REASON. Sure. A digital code is just a code where the information comes in separate bits, or *letters*. Take writing. I bet a smart guy like you knows how to write. In English, at every position, you either have a space, one of twenty-six letters, or a punctuation mark.

DOUBT. Human beings invented writing and computers. We didn't put code in living creatures. Are you saying human beings didn't invent code?

REASON. I am. All life has DNA code, plus technology to read the code and do all of life's work.

DOUBT. How did that happen?

REASON. Good question! Maybe we can talk about it later.

DOUBT. What does DNA code do?

REASON. It runs life. It builds life. Some sections of the code, called *genes*, contain instructions on how to build necessary parts, called *proteins*.

DNA—short for **deoxyribonucleic acid, is the molecule that contains the genetic code of organisms.**

Gene—**a section of DNA that contains instructions to build a protein.**

Protein—**a molecule formed by snapping together chains of life's twenty amino acids. A protein is like a machine part of life.**

DOUBT. How can code build anything?

REASON. Ever hear of 3-D printers?

DOUBT. 3-D printers are awesome. They use computer code to build three-dimensional objects.

REASON. Nice. You are smart.

DOUBT. Einstein.

REASON. That's why I knew you'd like the numbers proof first.

DOUBT. Flattery will get you nowhere. How does life use DNA?

REASON. All life has 3-D printers that read code to build parts.

DOUBT. What? All life, even simple life, has 3-D printers—these advanced machines?

REASON. Yes. You're not as dumb as you look.

DOUBT. That's a compliment, right? How does that work?

REASON. I like a technical person. Life's 3-D printers read the code three *letters* at a time to pick out one of twenty building blocks of life. These groups—three DNA *letters*—are called *codons*.

DOUBT. A codon is used to pick out a building block?

REASON. Yes. These building blocks are called amino acids. They have a central carbon atom, so they can be snapped together, like plastic blocks a child plays with.

Codon—a group of three *letters* of DNA.

Amino acid—a group of atoms that contains a carboxyl group, with carbon, oxygen, and hydrogen atoms, and an amino group with nitrogen and hydrogen atoms.

DOUBT. Details, details. Okay, life reads DNA one codon—three *letters*—at a time and picks out one of twenty special building blocks—special groups of atoms—called amino acids.[1] Are there only twenty amino acids?

REASON. No, there are hundreds. Life uses twenty special ones and snaps them together in chains to build proteins. There is overwhelming evidence these twenty were chosen by design.[2]

DOUBT. Wait. You said there are four different *letters* of DNA, right?

REASON. Yes. Four different groups of atoms that are the *letters* of DNA code.

DOUBT. Then, if I'm reading that code three *letters* at a time, there are four times four times four equals sixty-four possible combinations, right?

---

[1] Amino acids are three-dimensional structures, and can be formed in one of two ways, which are mirror images of each other. In life, if you take the amino acid and put the lone hydrogen atom at the top of the central carbon atom, the direction from the amino acid group to the carboxyl group almost always forms a left-handed molecule. There is no law of physics that prefers one of these shapes over the other. Yet almost all of the amino acids used in living organisms are left handed.

[2] A 2011 study by two NASA scientists compared life's *standard alphabet* of twenty amino acids to one million alternative sets (each also with twenty members) drawn randomly from a pool of fifty plausible candidates. They found "the standard alphabet exhibits better coverage (i.e., greater breadth and greater evenness) than any random set." They concluded "The standard set of twenty amino acids represents the possible spectra of size, charge, and hydrophobicity [aversion to water] more broadly and more evenly than can be explained by chance alone."

REASON. Correct, you are a math genius.

DOUBT. Einstein.

REASON. I see the resemblance.

DOUBT. That doesn't match up. If there are sixty-four possible combinations/codons, how do you code for just twenty amino acids? How does life know what codon means what amino acid, what snap on block?

REASON. Great question. That knowledge is prewired into every form of life. The design is magnificent. It automatically corrects many errors. Most amino acids can be specified by more than one codon.[3] Others tell the 3-D printer to stop.

DOUBT. Okay. Life's 3-D printer reads the first codon and picks out one of twenty special amino acids. Then what?

REASON. It reads the next codon, figures out which amino acid is specified by that codon, grabs that second amino acid, and literally snaps it onto the first amino acid, the first building block.[4]

---

[3] By the choice of which codon is used, there is sometimes a hidden second code.

[4] It takes incredible design to build an atomic machine to read three letters of DNA code and know which building block to pick, and to have those building blocks in reserve so you can snap on the correct one. This machine is in *all* life—it didn't develop gradually and it didn't arise by chance.

> *Warning!* **This book oversimplifies the technology of life. Life's technology is more complex than this (or any other) book can describe. Advanced technology requires a designer.**

DOUBT. Like plastic connecting blocks?

REASON. Yes. It takes energy to snap them together.

DOUBT. And the 3-D printer keeps going until it reaches a codon that tells it to stop, is that it?

REASON. I don't know how you figured that out, but yes. This chain of amino acids is called a protein.

DOUBT. Cool. How long is a typical protein, how many building blocks snapped together?

REASON. Depends. Simple proteins might have 150 amino acids or even less. Your muscles have proteins made up of over 34,000 amino acids linked together and folded into springs that allow you to move.[5] Human proteins often have three or four hundred amino acids snapped together.

---

[5] Human beings have a protein in their muscles called "Titin." Titin is the largest human protein, with 34,350 amino acids snapped together, a molecular weight equal to 3.8 million hydrogen atoms, and a structure that resembles a spring. To get the code to build titan, genetic machines cut out and carefully splice together 363 sections of DNA information. (Humans have an advanced processing system.) This is science fact. The theory that this all arose by chance is science fiction.

DOUBT. These chains of snap-together building blocks, these chains of amino acids with twenty possible choices at each position, are another type of digital code, aren't they?

REASON. Yes.

DOUBT. Similar to writing, I think. In writing, at each place, you have twenty-six possible letters, plus spaces, plus punctuation. In chains of amino acids, you have twenty choices.

REASON. Nice! You are Einstein. I think you get the idea of a digital code.

DOUBT. So some DNA code is used to build parts—build proteins out of amino acids. What does the rest do?

REASON. Some DNA code tells your body when to build a new part. Some DNA code tells your body how to put the parts together. Some DNA code tells how and when to turn the systems in your body on and off.

DOUBT. You're kidding, right? Who says that?

REASON. ENCODE.

DOUBT. N-what?

REASON. ENCODE.[6] Over four hundred top scientists working to decipher human DNA.

---

[6] ENCODE is an international collaboration of over 400 top scientists, working together, with no religious agenda, "to build a comprehensive parts list of functional elements in the human genome." In 2012, they simultaneously released 30 major papers. The front page of the *New York Times* announced. "The human genome is packed with at least four million gene switches that

DOUBT. Guess I missed that news flash. What did they find?

REASON. Lots. We have four million sections of DNA, four million sections of code, that are switches to turn our systems on and off.

DOUBT. I have four million switches in me?

REASON. Yes.

DOUBT. So I'm pretty special, right?

REASON. Very special. A piece of work.

DOUBT. Alright, I have lots of DNA code. How much did you say?

REASON. I didn't. Maybe 3.2 billion (3,200,000,000) *letters* of DNA code in almost all of your maybe thirty trillion (30,000,000,000,000) cells.

DOUBT. Wow! You like big numbers.

REASON. These *fantastically* big numbers point to God.

DOUBT. Do all scientists agree life runs code?

REASON. Absolutely! One hundred percent! DNA is the most complex code ever! Code that builds all the parts, tells how to put them together, and tells how to operate life!

DOUBT. Calm down. Okay, so there's code in us and in all life. What was your second point, something about you can't really get working code by chance?

---

reside in bits of DNA that once were dismissed as 'junk' but that turn out to play critical roles in controlling how cells, organs and other tissues behave."

Step 2: You Can't Really Get Working Code by Chance

REASON. Yes. You can't get the code—

DOUBT. Nonsense! If I type randomly, won't I eventually type everything?

REASON. Are we talking fantasy or reality here?

DOUBT. Reality.

REASON. Then, no, not really. Here's a quote special for you. "What a piece of work is a man, how noble in reason, how infinite in faculties, in form and moving how express and admirable, in action how like an angel, in apprehension how like a god!"

> **What a piece of work is a man, how noble in reason, how infinite in faculties, in form and moving how express and admirable, in action how like an angel, in apprehension how like a god!**
> **—This phrase is specified by 185 places where each place is a letter, a space, a comma, or an exclamation mark.**

DOUBT. You and your quotes. Who said that?

REASON. William Shakespeare. Lived in England more than 400 years ago.

DOUBT. Is there a point here?

REASON. Imagine you peck away blindly at a typewriter, waiting for that phrase to appear.

DOUBT. Are you comparing me to a blind chicken?

REASON. Never! Don't be silly! You are more intelligent than a chicken.

DOUBT. Not sure I appreciate these compliments. How long before that Shakespeare phrase is likely to appear?

REASON. A long time. Let's give you help.

DOUBT. Good. I need help.

REASON. No comment. Suppose every atom in the universe is also a blind chicken pecking at a typewriter.

DOUBT. Wow! How many atoms is that?

REASON. No one knows. Let's say 10^{90}. A number with 90 zeros, a million trillion, trillion, trillion, trillion, trillion, trillion, trillion chickens. And suppose each of these atoms/chickens is typing as fast as is theoretically possible, about 10^{44} letters a second.

DOUBT. How fast is that?

REASON. Fast enough to type each second a pile of books one hundred million miles in diameter—a ball of books too big to fit between the Earth and the Sun.

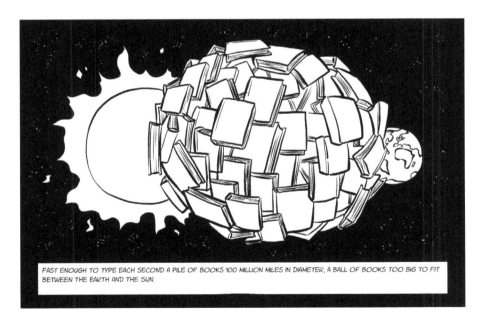

FAST ENOUGH TO TYPE EACH SECOND A PILE OF BOOKS 100 MILLION MILES IN DIAMETER, A BALL OF BOOKS TOO BIG TO FIT BETWEEN THE EARTH AND THE SUN.

DOUBT. You're kidding, right? Each atom in the universe, which we're imagining is a chicken, types that many books every second?

REASON. That's the picture.

DOUBT. Then this is easy! Me and my gazillion atom/ chicken friends typing that fast are going to bang out that Shakespeare phrase millions of times in a fraction of a second, right?

REASON. Not exactly.

DOUBT. What is *not exactly?* How long?

REASON. If you all type for a trillion, trillion years, and don't take any bathroom breaks, you still have an almost unimaginably small chance that you or any of your atom/chicken friends would *ever* type that phrase.

DOUBT. What? More of your big numbers! You cannot be serious.

REASON. I am.

DOUBT. How can that be?

REASON. Remember the phrase started "What a piece of work…" Look at that first letter, the *w* in the first word, the *w* in *what*. If you're typing randomly, blindly, no peeking at the keys, what are the chances you hit a *w?*

DOUBT. One in twenty-six?

REASON. Close. Don't forget there are also spaces and punctuation. Let's say just twenty-nine choices for each spot—twenty-six letters, a space, a comma, or an exclamation mark.

DOUBT. Okay, twenty-nine choices for each spot.

REASON. So what are the chances you'll type the first two letters right, the *w* and the *h*?

DOUBT. That's easy. If there are twenty-nine choices at each spot, then there are twenty-nine times twenty-nine different possibilities for the first two spots, so my chances are one in twenty-nine times twenty-nine. (Checks calculator.) My calculator says that's 841.

REASON. Genius! That proves it. We're done here. End of story.

DOUBT. What? How does that prove anything?

REASON. *Keep going.* Multiply by twenty-nine for each spot for *each* of the 185 letters/spaces/punctuation marks in the phrase. You'll get a *fantastically* big number, a number so big that, even with all those chickens typing super, super fast for a trillion, trillion years, the odds that this Shakespeare phrase will ever appear, anywhere in all those books, are still impossibly small.

> **Odds of getting**
>
> **First 5 letters/places right ≈ 1 in 20 million**
>
> **First 10 letters/places right ≈ 1 in 420 million, million**
>
> **First 25 letters/places right ≈ 1 in 3 trillion, trillion, trillion (10^{36})**
>
> **First 100 letters/places right ≈ 1 in 10^{146}**
>
> **All 185 letters/places right ≈ 1 in 10^{270}**

DOUBT. Hmmm. (Thinks about it a minute.) You're right. If you multiply twenty-nine by itself 185 times, you get a *really* big number.

REASON. So big it's hard to imagine. A *fantastically* big number. Also, that phrase isn't that long.

DOUBT. You're right. The instructions for building a machine would be much longer.

REASON. And even if that Shakespeare phrase did appear, how would you ever find it?

DOUBT. Good point. Well, the math's right, but it seems strange. What's going on?

REASON. You hit the *probability wall.*

DOUBT. The what?

REASON. The probability wall. There were too many possibilities, and you didn't have enough time or chances to get over the wall.

DOUBT. Explain.

REASON. Love to. This is key. Think of low probabilities as walls you have to get over. The lower the probability, the harder it is to get something right, the higher the wall. Each time the probability gets ten times lower, we'll say the wall gets one foot higher. Ever see a bike lock with a combination?

DOUBT. Yeah! Mine has four dials, with ten positions on each dial, zero to nine.

REASON. Imagine each of those dials, each one out of ten chance, raises the wall one foot. Now, how many possible combinations?

DOUBT. I can do this. With ten choices for each dial, and four dials, where each can spin separately, you have ten times ten times ten times ten equals 10,000 possible combinations.

REASON. Nice! With one dial—a one in ten chance—the probability wall is one foot high. With four dials, a one in 10,000 chance of getting it right by accident, the probability wall is four feet high. Now suppose a thief tries to open the lock, tries to get over that wall. What are his chances?

| 1 IN 10,000 = 10^4 | 1 IN 1,000,000 = 10^6 | 1 IN 1,000,000,000 = 10^9 |

DOUBT. Not good, if he doesn't know the code that works, the one combination that opens the lock.

REASON. Right. It's not easy to get over a probability wall four feet high. But suppose the thief tries 1,000 times. There's three zeros in 1,000, so that creates an opportunity ladder three feet high. With 1,000 attempts, the thief climbs the opportunity ladder three feet, and only has one foot to go, a one in ten chance of opening the lock.

DOUBT. Got it.

REASON. So even with 1,000 tries, the thief is still not likely to open the lock by chance. Even with 1,000 tries, his chances are one in ten. But if a group of thieves came by, and each tried 1,000 times, you'd probably lose your bike.

DOUBT. Right. More chances. The thieves together have a higher opportunity ladder, more likely to get over the probability wall.

REASON. Exactly. Now imagine a bigger lock. Imagine 185 dials, and each dial has twenty-nine possibilities, and again the dials can spin separately so any possible combination can appear.

DOUBT. Whoa! That's a big lock! So you're imagining that Shakespeare phrase as a bike lock where each letter/ space/punctuation mark is like a separate dial with twenty-nine possibilities? One hundred eighty-five spinning dials with twenty-nine choices on each dial?

REASON. Yes! That lock creates a probability wall 270 feet high. I gave you an opportunity ladder bigger than anything the universe could possibly offer, with every atom in the universe trying 10^{44} combinations every second for a trillion, trillion years, but the ladder fell far short. Over 110 feet short.[7]

---

[7] Odds of opening lock with one chance = 1 in 29^{185} = 1 in 3.5 x 10^{270} (probability wall about 270 feet high). Number of chances = 10^{90} atoms x 10^{44} chances per second x 3 x 10^7 seconds per year x 10^{24} years = 3 x 10^{156} (opportunity ladder about 156 feet high). Odds of opening lock with all those chances about 1 in 10^{114} (top of ladder is 114 feet below top of wall).

DOUBT. I think I get it. Too many choices, not enough time.

REASON. All we did was multiply, no fancy math.

DOUBT. That's crazy! Not that long a quote, but the whole universe has no real chance of opening the lock. I'm shocked. Numbers get big fast when you multiply.

REASON. That's my point! Numbers get *fantastically* big, far beyond the ability of random events to open the lock. So you see you can't accidentally get a specific section of new code, other than a very short code, by random actions. Not really. Maybe once if you got ridiculously unbelievably lucky, but not over and over, that's for sure.

DOUBT. I see that, but maybe you don't need to get it perfectly right. What if there are lots of codes that work? DNA codes build parts. Maybe it's not likely an exact code will appear by chance, but maybe there are lots of codes that will build what that kind of animal needs. Why doesn't that mess up your proof?

REASON. Good question! Seriously! When DNA was discovered, scientists knew that getting a specific code by chance was just about mathematically impossible. They originally thought lots of different codes might work.

DOUBT. Were they right?

REASON. No. Scientists have found that getting *any* new working DNA code by chance, not just a specific working code, is mathematically still close to impossible. The odds against getting lucky by chance are still *fantastic*.

DOUBT. Why?

REASON. Because the building blocks, the amino acids in the chain, have to fold in just the right way to be useful, to be a useful part in the machinery of life. It's like language. It's hard to get the letters and spaces to form words and also follow a sentence structure.

DOUBT. Tell me more.

REASON. Sure. I'll show you by analogy to written language, and then we'll talk about experimental results. Suppose you have some random sequence of one hundred English letters and spaces. What do you think are the odds it makes real words and basic grammatical sense?

DOUBT. You mean looks and sounds like real language, even if it is meaningless?

REASON. That's it. How likely?

DOUBT. From your tone, I'm thinking not likely.

REASON. Good guess. The odds are much worse than one in a number with one hundred *zeros*. That's less than the odds of closing your eyes and picking one special marked marble out of a pile of marbles as big as the known universe. The probability wall to get one hundred random English letters and spaces to make real words and basic grammatical sense is over one hundred feet high.

DOUBT. Why so rare?

REASON. Because you not only have to get real words by chance, they have to fit the English language.

DOUBT. What about chains of amino acids, the building blocks that build proteins? Any experimental results?

REASON. Yes. The first was buried in a 1982 paper by two scientists from MIT.

DOUBT. MIT? I was going to go there.

REASON. What's the problem? One study rated it the world's top university.

DOUBT. Not for me. Not highly rated for football.

REASON. It's important to know what's important. Anyhow, these MIT guys estimated the chances that a short amino acid sequence, of just ninety-two amino acids, would build a particular protein, a particular working part of life.

DOUBT. Well? Come on, what were the odds?

REASON. About one in a number with sixty-three *zeros*, one in 10^{63}. A probability wall sixty-three feet high.

DOUBT. That's pretty small, huh?

REASON. Afraid so.

DOUBT. How small?

REASON. *Fantastically* small. Get out of town not even close small. They found that scrambling up a sequence of ninety-two amino acids and getting a protein—a particular machine part of life—that did the same job was about equal to your chances of picking a special marked marble out of a pile of marbles 1,000 light years[8] in diameter.

---

[8] A *light year* is the distance light travels in one year, which is about 6 trillion (6,000,000,000,000) miles. One thousand light years is about 6,000 trillion miles.

That's 6,000 trillion miles in diameter. A pile of marbles that, if centered at the Earth, would include thousands of stars. A probability wall sixty-three feet high!

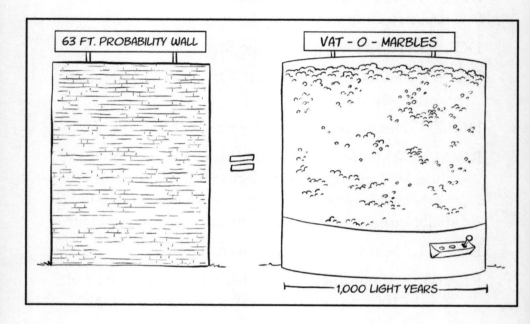

DOUBT. Double whoa! Do the odds of getting a working protein get better as the protein gets bigger?

REASON. No. They get worse. *Much* worse. Another scientist found that the odds of scrambling 150 amino acids and getting *any* sort of useful protein, *any* even potentially useful machine part of life, are about one in 10^{74}—one in a number with seventy-four *zeros*. Two other experiments got roughly similar results.

DOUBT. One in seventy-four doesn't seem like impossible odds.

REASON. No, it's one in a number with seventy-four *zeros*, a probability wall seventy-four feet high! I can give you an example to show how rare that is, how impossible it is to get over a probability wall seventy-four feet high.

DOUBT. Alright, what?

REASON. Imagine you drop a pin on a piece of paper and measure the odds of randomly landing on a tiny dot. Suppose you make the paper big enough and the dot small enough that your chances of randomly dropping the pin on that dot are one in a number with seventy-four *zeros*. To say the same thing, you make the paper big enough and the dot small enough so the probability wall of hitting the dot is seventy-four feet high.

DOUBT. So the paper would be as big as a football field, maybe?

REASON. Bigger. Bigger than the known universe. If you made the paper 200 billion light years[9] on each side, and made the dot as small as a single carbon atom, so tiny you could fit twenty-five trillion of them into a square millimeter, then your chance of randomly dropping the pin, and hitting that special dot, is one in a number with seventy-four *zeros*. That's how hard it is to get over a seventy-four-foot probability wall by chance.

DOUBT. Wow!

REASON. This piece of paper is so big that, if you randomly drop a pin every second for your entire life, it's not likely one pin would land inside our galaxy.

---

[9] Two hundred billion light years is about 1,200 billion trillion miles.

DOUBT. Double wow!

REASON. And the dot is so small that, even if you randomly dropped pins on a space equal to the head of a needle every second for your entire life, it's not likely you would ever hit the dot.

DOUBT. Triple wow!

REASON. Point is, there haven't been enough events, enough pin drops if you will, in the history of life on earth to ever hit that tiny dot. A number with seventy-four *zeros* is a *fantastically* big number, and the odds are too heavy to expect to ever overcome that by chance. The probability wall is too high. There haven't been that many new amino acid codes—changes caused by mutations—in the entire history of life on Earth.[10]

DOUBT. So, relatively speaking, it is unbelievably rare for a random sequence of amino acids to create any sort of new working protein, is that what you're saying?

REASON. Yes. Just as it is unbelievably rare for a random sequence of English letters and spaces to spell real words and make grammatical sense. These numbers with sixty zeros, or seventy zeros, are *fantastically*

---

[10] Estimates for the number of organisms that have ever lived are usually below 10^{30}. The vast majority of these are bacteria or other creatures with one cell, and they don't live very long, but let's be generous and say 1,000 mutations for each. That gives a number with thirty-three zeros for the number of mutations ever, an opportunity ladder thirty-three feet high. Even that is still way, way short of a seventy-four-foot probability wall.

big. You can't beat these odds. In the real world, you cannot get over a probability wall sixty or seventy feet high. Yes, it is possible, and you can imagine getting lucky, like winning some impossible lottery, but it's not going to happen over and over again, that's for sure. New working proteins are like rare jewels, jewels so rare you would not expect to find even one if you mined every planet in the universe, yet scientists have found hundreds, sometimes thousands, of these jewels in every creature on earth.

DOUBT. Okay, you can't get working DNA code by chance, not really. But that doesn't prove God is real.

REASON. Good point Einstein. You broke my proof into three steps. It's just step two.

DOUBT. Bring it on. So step one is all life runs code. Step two is you can't really get working code by chance. What's step three?

Step 3: Every Kind of Animal Has New and Unique Working Code

REASON. Every kind of animal has working code that is new and unique, that appears only in the DNA of that kind of animal, that doesn't resemble the code in any other kind of animal.

DOUBT. Explain.

REASON. Imagine there's a book for each kind of animal. This book contains all the code to build and run that animal.

DOUBT. So the DNA code for each animal is like a book, is that it?

REASON. Bingo!

DOUBT. Big book or little book?

REASON. Ha-ha! Depends, but bigger than you might think. For human beings, the *book* is like a thousand thick volumes. Believe it or not, for a few animals and plants, it's thirty or forty thousand thick volumes. Even for the smallest one-cell organisms—what we might naively think of as *simple* or *primitive* life—it's typically thousands of pages.

E. Coli ≈ 4.6 million DNA letters

Mouse ≈ 2.7 billion DNA letters

Human ≈ 3.2 billion DNA letters

Paris japonica (Japanese flower) ≈ 149 billion DNA letters

DOUBT. Okay, the DNA code is like a book, and there's a different book for each kind of animal. Then what?

REASON. Each book contains completely new sections, unique paragraphs or even chapters that are not related to *any* other paragraph or chapter in *any* of the other books.

DOUBT. So you can't just tweak a few letters or spaces and change that paragraph or chapter into any other paragraph or chapter in *any* of the millions of these so-called *books* for other kinds of animals, is that what you're saying?

REASON. Exactly! Every kind of animal contains sections of completely new working code that do not resemble any other section of working code in any other kind of animal. Chickens have special chicken working code. Cats have special cat working code. You can't get the code of life—

DOUBT. What does the new code do?

REASON. Lots of things. Usually things that make that animal special. The code in jellyfish to build toxins is new code not found in any other kind of animal. Humans have fifty-four unique, one-of-a-kind codes to build parts for our brains.

DOUBT. Whoa! Give me another example.

REASON. Ever see an octopus?

DOUBT. In the aquarium. Eight legs, right? Weird. Kind of scary.

REASON. That's the beast. Octopuses have eight legs, three hearts, and can taste through the suckers on their legs. They have parts of their brains in their legs. In 2015, scientists found that the code for an octopus is so shockingly different from other species that it was like an alien creature from outer space.

DOUBT. Octopuses are aliens? Were they serious?

REASON. No, they were just astonished at how different the code was from anything they had ever seen. Ever hear of the leafcutter ant?

DOUBT. Not sure. Ants?

REASON. Next to human beings, leafcutter ants have the most complex societies on Earth. In a few years, they can build a colony of eight million ants, with four different body—

DOUBT. Blah blah blah. Ants are bugs. I don't like bugs.

REASON. Okay, TMI. Here's the point. Most of the protein-building DNA in a leafcutter ant is brand-new code not in any other kind of animal. Leafcutter ants have over 9,000 unique genes, unique sections of code to build proteins—parts—not found in any other kind of animal.

DOUBT. That's a lot. What's a typical percentage?

REASON. Hard to measure. We still don't know what a lot of the code does, so scientists tend to focus on those sections of the code that life's 3-D printers use to build parts. Those sections are called *genes*. Each gene contains instructions for life's 3-D printers to snap together amino acids and assemble a *protein*. Scientists have found that typically about 10 percent of the genes of an animal, the protein-building DNA codes, are brand-new code for that kind of animal only.

DOUBT. Were they surprised?

REASON. You bet! Blown away!

DOUBT. Why?

REASON. Under Darwin's theory, new code results from random, gradual, one-at-a-time accidents. You never get completely new sections of working code. So when these new unrelated genes were discovered, scientists called them *orphan genes*.

> **Comparative genome analyses indicate that every taxonomic group so far studied contains 10-20 percent of genes that lack recognizable homologs [similar counterparts] in other species.**
> *—Trends in Genetics* **2009**
>
> **Orphan genes have since been found in every genome sequenced to date, from mosquito to man, roundworm to rat, and their members are still growing.**
> *—New Scientist* **2014**

DOUBT. Why?

REASON. No known relatives. The code for these genes didn't look like the code for *any* other genes in *any* other kind of animal. They were *orphans*. No parents, no way to know or even guess where they came from. No similar sections of DNA code in *any* other creature, so they called the genes *orphans*. I call them *designer* genes.

> *Designer gene*—a gene (section of DNA coding that builds a protein) that does not resemble any other gene in any other kind of animal. These genes are more commonly known as *"orphan genes,"* because they have no known relatives. *Designer genes/orphan genes* contradict Darwin's theory that new species came from a series of mistakes.

DOUBT. That's cute. Nerdy, but cute. Okay. Each kind of animal has a *book* of code in its DNA, and each kind of animal has major sections of new code. But some people say DNA is mostly junk.

REASON. Nonsense! It's such amazing code, so complicated, that we still don't know what a lot of it does! Just because we can't figure it out doesn't mean it's junk!

DOUBT. Calm down. What do scientists say?

REASON. Those 400-plus ENCODE scientists announced, when they released thirty major papers worldwide, that perhaps 80 percent of DNA code serves a purpose. Their lead guy said "it's likely 80 percent will go to 100 percent."

> **"It's likely that 80 percent will go to 100 percent," stated one of ENCODE's top researchers. "We don't really have any large chunks of redundant DNA. This metaphor of junk isn't that useful."**
> **—*Discover* 2012**

DOUBT. Got it, not junk. But maybe it came about by chance?

REASON. You can't get new working code by chance! You can't get over the probability wall, remember?

DOUBT. Not even over billions of years?

REASON. Not even if you imagine trillions times trillions of years!

DOUBT. Where are we on your numbers proof?

REASON. Done! We've done all three steps. One, all life runs code! Two, you can't really get new working code by chance! Three, every kind of animal contains new, unique, working code!

1. ALL LIFE RUNS CODE.

2. YOU CAN'T REALLY GET NEW WORKING CODE BY CHANCE.

3. EVERY KIND OF ANIMAL HAS WORKING CODE THAT IS NEW AND UNIQUE, THAT DOESN'T RESEMBLE THE CODE IN ANY OTHER KIND OF ANIMAL.

REASON. *I proved the existence of God!* Drum roll please! Applause! Standing ovation!

DOUBT. Sit down. Seems crazy. Your first point, that life runs code, you're saying that is now universally accepted by all scientists?

REASON. Yes. The code is in the DNA. Or you can look at the code of amino acids in proteins, the code of the building blocks snapped together. The two codes are related.

DOUBT. Your second point, that you can't really get new working code by chance, you claim that's supported by experiments and makes sense when you consider the rarity of getting an English sentence by chance?

REASON. Absolutely. The experimental evidence shows a rarity that's hard to comprehend. New working proteins are *fantastically* rare. The probability wall to get one by chance is *fantastically* high.

DOUBT. But anything can happen, right?

REASON. Right. But with these ridiculous odds against it ever happening once, against ever opening the lock, against every dropping the pin exactly on that super tiny dot, there is no way it happened by chance thousands and thousands of times to form every kind of animal. In the real world, *fantastically* hard locks cannot be opened. You can't get over the probability wall.

DOUBT. Your third point, that every kind of animal contains new, unique working code, code that doesn't resemble the code in any other kind of animal—like a new paragraph or chapter in the book of that animal—this is accepted science?

REASON. Yes. It has been repeatedly verified and reported in major scientific journals. We humans have fifty-four special DNA codes just to build parts needed in our brains—fifty-four complex, unique designer genes that don't resemble *any* genes in *any* other animal, just to build our brains. The pin dropped on the exact right dot at least fifty-four times to form our brains, and that's only the odds of getting an average length working protein, not the highly complex proteins of our brains.

Humans have at least 54 complex designer genes to build parts in our brains.

DOUBT. That's amazing. There are fifty-four unique codes—orphan/designer genes—just to build parts in our brains?

REASON. Yes! Each has a *fantastically* high probability wall.

DOUBT. But if you've got new, unique working code, that just proves different kinds of animals didn't arise by chance. It doesn't prove God is real.

REASON. You don't think this proves God is real?

DOUBT. I don't.

REASON. Let's get some coffee.

[After a few moments]

DOUBT. Alright, tell me again why this proves God is real.

REASON. *No other explanation.* Science *proves* chance is impossible. Remember what Sherlock Holmes said, "When you have eliminated the impossible, whatever remains, however improbable, must be the truth?"

"WHEN YOU HAVE ELIMINATED THE IMPOSSIBLE, WHATEVER REMAINS, HOWEVER IMPROBABLE, MUST BE THE TRUTH."

- SHERLOCK HOLMES

DOUBT. I'm not sure about Sherlock. Probably not even a real person.

REASON. Ha! There are only two ways of getting working code. One is chance and the other is design. Either a mind designed the code, or it arose by chance. Chance doesn't work, the odds are too heavy, the locks are *fantastically* hard to open. The probability walls are too high. So the code was designed, created by a mind.

DOUBT. Couldn't there be some other explanation?

REASON. No! In all of science, in all of history, and throughout all human experience, the only known source for working code is from a mind. Working code contains information, and information can only come from a mind. Ever hear of SETI?

> **In all of science, in all of history, and throughout all human experience, the only known source for working code is from a mind.**

DOUBT. C-what?

REASON. SETI. Search for extraterrestrial intelligence —aliens.

DOUBT. Aliens! I'm a *Star Wars* fan. Seen *every* movie. What's looking for aliens got to do with working code?

REASON. That's how people have been looking for aliens. People have been listening to space for over fifty years, hoping to discover signals that contain a working code, something that could not have arisen by chance. Ever see a movie called *Contact?*

DOUBT. Don't think so.

REASON. Came out in 1997. Science fiction. Jodie Foster played a scientist who discovers a signal from outer space that contains working code.

DOUBT. What was in the code?

REASON. First, they discovered a sequence of prime numbers. Then instructions for building a machine. Because this working code couldn't have arisen by chance, then, in this fantasy movie, they knew it came from a mind. It contained information.

DOUBT. So your point is?

REASON. My point is working code *must* come from a mind. DNA is code. We now know every kind of animal has brand-new sections of working code, massive amounts of new information. In the real world, you can't get it by chance.

DOUBT. I don't know.

REASON. Do you have a smartphone?

DOUBT. Yes.

REASON. Suppose you want to get your smartphone to do something new, something it cannot presently do. How do you do that?

DOUBT. Easy. Download the app.

REASON. What's an *app?*

DOUBT. Programing. Instructions.

REASON. Which are?

DOUBT. I see your point. An app is new code.

REASON. Exactly! Life works the same way. For a kind of animal to do something new, it has to have new code, new apps.

DOUBT. Maybe we will discover some new type of science to explain this.

REASON. Ha! Science of the gaps, heh? Science isn't a magic wand. Science is figuring stuff out. We know the laws of chemistry and physics very well. DNA sections and amino acids can't magically get in the right order. It takes a mind.

DOUBT. Like it takes a mind to build an app?

REASON. You got it. How many apps are there for your cell phone?

DOUBT. I don't know. Thousands, for sure.

REASON. How many of those were created by chance, by accidently messed-up code that just happened to do something completely new?

DOUBT. I'd say none.

REASON. Only a mind can create a new app for your cell phone, and only a mind can create a new app for life, something that helps create a different kind of animal.

DOUBT. Maybe there is some other way to create working DNA code, or the codes of amino acids?

REASON. Get real. In all of science, in all of history, and in all of human experience, only a mind can create working code.

DOUBT. Then why don't people get that?

REASON. You tell me. The irony is we live in a digital age, an age with marvelous digital code everywhere, and we know all that code, every app, every website, every program, was created by a mind. Yet when we encounter the most advanced code we have ever seen, a code so advanced and complex we are just beginning to understand it, the code of DNA, a code that builds technology far more advanced than human technology, we think it arose by chance. It's the greatest delusion in history.

DOUBT. You say DNA is not just code but advanced code?

REASON. Absolutely! It has at least two levels of information.

DOUBT. Who says that?

REASON. ENCODE. Those 400-plus top scientists. And a lot of DNA code can be read on multiple levels, sometimes even backward and forward, sometimes as overlapping code. Do you know any human code that can do that?

DOUBT. Not that I've ever heard of. Wow! A code with multiple layers of information that sometimes you can read both backward and forward. That has to be designed. How can scientists—educated people who know about DNA—refuse to accept this?

REASON. They're starting to. The facts are forcing them. In 2016, at a meeting of the prestigious Royal Society in England, the top evolutionary biologists in the world got together to try to solve the problem, to try to explain, without God, where all this working code—all this biological information—came from. They failed.

> **There is no known law of physics able to create information from nothing.**
> **—Paul Davies, Physicist**

DOUBT. This proves an intelligence, a super intelligence, has created every kind of animal?

REASON. Yes. Especially human beings. We are not here by chance. Science *proves* there is a God.

DOUBT. *Wow!* I think I finally get it.

REASON. Alleluia! Thanks be to God. I knew you were smart.

DOUBT. Can I ask you a question?

REASON. Sure.

DOUBT. Is what you are saying, your basic point, that you can't get the code of life by chance?

REASON. Yes.

DOUBT. Why didn't you just say that?

The Common Sense Proof

DOUBT. You can prove God three ways?

REASON. Yes.

DOUBT. I was trying to explain your numbers proof to a friend, but I got confused. Do you have a simpler proof?

REASON. I think so. Let's use common sense.

DOUBT. That'd be perfect. How can common sense show us God?

REASON. Do you like technology?

DOUBT. *Love* technology! Computers, smartphones, internet! Cars, planes, spaceships! We're talking video games!

REASON. Human beings created all that, right?

DOUBT. I thought you were smart. Of course!

REASON. What is *the* most advanced technology?

DOUBT. I don't know. Hard to say whether the internet is more advanced than a spaceship.

REASON. Let me suggest something much more advanced.

DOUBT. What?

REASON. The human brain.

DOUBT. That's not technology, that's life!

REASON. Life runs on technology, remember? DNA code builds machinery!

DOUBT. I never thought of it that way. Of course the human brain is technology.

REASON. Consider all it can do. With your brain, you control, to an astonishing degree, over 600 muscles. You can perform coordinated feats, like standing upright.

DOUBT. What's so hard about standing?

REASON. It took you a year to learn how to do it. Now your brain balances so well you usually don't even think about it.

DOUBT. I guess that is amazing.

REASON. Your brain can access memory banks of your life and what you have learned. You have the gift of reason, of being able to figure things out. With training, people can perform dazzling feats, like playing difficult piano pieces from memory, or playing chess blindfolded.

DOUBT. How does the brain do that?

REASON. Great question. *No one knows!*

No one knows the details of how the human brain works. No one really knows how it processes information, why we feel emotions, how memories are stored, or why we are conscious. The human brain is too complex to have arisen by chance.

DOUBT. People can't figure out how the brain works?

REASON. Not much is known. In 2017, researchers found the brain builds complex structures to solve problems. One scientist found tens of millions of complex structures in a small speck of the brain, connected through seven dimensions.

The neurons in the network react to stimuli in an extremely organized manner. We found a world we never imagined. There are tens of millions of these objects even in a small speck of the brain, up through seven dimensions. In some networks, we even found structures with up to eleven dimensions.
—*Journal of Computational Neuroscience* 2017

DOUBT. Watch the quotes. The brain builds structures to solve problems?

REASON. That's the scientific evidence. Maybe that's why, when you do something over and over, you get better at it. Maybe the brain gets better at building the structures you need.

DOUBT. Tens of millions of structures in a small speck? Awesome! But what you said about dimensions makes no sense.

REASON. When the researcher talks about dimensions, he is really talking about degrees of connectivity. If seven neurons are connected to each other, he is calling that a seven-dimensional structure.

DOUBT. What's a neuron?

REASON. A nerve cell in the brain.

DOUBT. How many neurons do I have?

REASON. About 100 billion, or 100,000,000,000. About the same number as stars in a galaxy. If you counted one number a second, it would take you three thousand years to count that high. A human baby grows an average of 2.5 million brain cells each minute while it is in the womb.

DOUBT. And these brain cells are connected?

REASON. Yes, through hundreds of trillions of synapses. You have as many connections as stars in thousands of galaxies. A single human brain has more information processing units than all the computers, routers, and internet connections on Earth. They communicate with light and with electricity. The memory capacity of your brain is in the same ballpark as the entire World Wide Web.

DOUBT. Double awesome! So it's all just jammed into our brains?

REASON. No, it's designed into our brains. Scientists have found the neurons are placed to minimize *connection costs*. The human brain is fantastically energy efficient. Human circuits would require 1,000 times more energy.

DOUBT. Sounds like that kind of design didn't happen by chance.

REASON. It didn't. Where does technology come from?

DOUBT. From a mind.

REASON. And would you agree the human brain is the most advanced technology anyone has ever found?

DOUBT. Seems I have to.

REASON. Then common sense tells us the human brain was designed, and God is real. There is *no other explanation*.

DOUBT. Amazing.

REASON. And here's a further thought.

DOUBT. Okay.

REASON. If your brain really was put together by a process of mistakes, why would you trust it?

DOUBT. You're right. I do trust my brain.

REASON. Let me give you another example. Remember that DNA has a code of four different groups of atoms? Remember that all life has machines, 3-D printers, that *read* the groups of atoms and pick out one of twenty special building blocks to snap onto a chain that becomes a protein, a useful part in life?

DOUBT. Yes.

REASON. How did that happen? How could any system this complex arise by chance?

DOUBT. Don't know.

REASON. Obviously, it couldn't. There is no way the technology of life came about by chance. It was designed. That's common sense.

DOUBT. Amen.

The Logic Proof

DOUBT. Using numbers, you've shown me you can't get technology by chance, and, using common sense, you've shown me you can't get technology by chance. Since there is no other explanation, you claim God is real. Does that all work logically?

REASON. Absolutely. Let's prove the existence of God with logic. Like in math class.

DOUBT. Cool!

REASON. Math has theorems, logical arguments that prove or disapprove statements. All theorems are based on unprovable assumptions. You always start by assuming some things are true, then you use that foundation to prove other things are true. What you can prove rests on, depends on, your starting truths. Your starting truths are the foundation you build on.

DOUBT. We saw that in geometry. We studied a Greek man named Euclid who lived thousands of years ago. He began with five starting truths—five postulates.

REASON. Super example. Before you can *prove* anything, you have to start with a foundation of things you assume are true. I'm going to prove the existence of God using logic, and I'm going to start with three assumed truths. If you accept all three of my assumed truths, my starting assumptions, then I will have proved God is real. Ready?

DOUBT. Hit me!

REASON. My first assumed truth is that there is an objective reality.

DOUBT. What does that mean?

REASON. Things are real. We are not in a computer simulation. Life is real, and this world is real.

DOUBT. You can't prove that?

REASON. Not really. You have to assume it. But if you don't agree things are real, you can't know or prove anything.

DOUBT. Seems obvious. I accept your first assumption. I accept things are real.

REASON. My second assumed truth is that our senses generally provide accurate information about reality, about our world.

DOUBT. What does that mean?

REASON. We can trust clear signals from our senses. If we run into a stone wall, we say that *proves* both that the wall exists and that it is hard. If scientists around the world find all living creatures contain coded groups of atoms we call DNA, we say that *proves* the existence of DNA.

DOUBT. Okay. Seems to me that if you don't trust what you see, what you touch and hear and smell, then you can't know anything either. You have to be careful sometimes, but I agree we can use our senses to learn about the world.

REASON. My third assumed truth is that if there is only one explanation for something, then that explanation is true.

DOUBT. Tell me more.

REASON. If we find something that has only one explanation, one cause, then that explanation and that cause are accurate. Suppose you put money in a safe. You lock it, but when you come back the next day the money is gone. What would you say is the explanation, the cause of the money not being there?

DOUBT. Somebody found a way to take my money!

REASON. You wouldn't say that perhaps the money just transported itself to a different universe?

DOUBT. Ha! In all of human experience, that has never happened. There is no scientific reason to think it could happen.

REASON. Maybe there is an invisible money-eating monster that got hungry?

DOUBT. Get real. If the money's gone, somebody, some person did it. There is no other known explanation. I wouldn't know how they did it, but I would know some person is responsible.

REASON. Agree. That's basically my third assumed truth. When there is only one known explanation for something, that explanation is true. When there is only one known reason why something happens, that reason is correct.

DOUBT. I can't argue with any of your assumptions. If all three aren't true, I don't see how I can know or prove anything. Now what?

REASON. Put them together. Using our senses, with careful observations, we have found *fantastic* technology in every living creature. Plants have sensors that detect detailed variations in both light and temperature. Some birds, fish, turtles, and even butterflies have sensors that detect both the direction and intensity of the Earth's magnetic field, coupled with navigation systems that allow them to travel thousands of miles and return to the same field, stream, beach, or tree. This technology is complex almost beyond imagination— much more advanced than anything humans have created. We are only beginning to understand how DNA code works, with overlapping layers of information.

DOUBT. That's incredible.

REASON. Using my first two assumed truths, I have now proved this technology is real. It exists in a real world.

DOUBT. I can't argue with that.

REASON. Great. Now, and here's the clincher, what's the explanation? Where did life's technology come from? In all of human history and experience, only an intelligent being can create technology. In all of science, there is no other known explanation for the existence of technology. Chance is pathetically inadequate. No one has ever seen new technology created by accident, and the odds against it ever happening by chance are *fantastic!* The probability walls are too high.

REASON. My logic proof is this. Scientists have found complex technology in every living creature. Life's technology is real. In all of human history, and in all of science, the only explanation for technology is that it came from a mind. Therefore, using my third assumed truth, the technology of life was designed. It was created by a mind. I call that designer God.

DOUBT. That sounds solid. Does everyone agree with your starting truths?

REASON. Almost everyone does, deep down. If you climb a mountain and come to the edge of a cliff thousands of feet high, you would, one, conclude there is such a thing as a cliff; two, trust your eyes the cliff is high; and three, believe gravity will pull you down, like it always pulls things down, if you step off.

DOUBT. Yes, if I walk to the edge of a high cliff, I will think the cliff is real. I will trust my eyes the cliff is high. And because, throughout all human history gravity pulls people down when they step off a cliff with no support, and because there is no scientific reason to think otherwise, I will conclude that if I step off, it will pull me down too.

REASON. Well said. Our society is in denial over God. We have climbed the mountain of science and see fantastic technology in living creatures. This technology is confirmed in multiple scientific articles every month. Yet people close their eyes and step off the cliff, into the spiritual and moral abyss of atheism.

DOUBT. Your three proofs are related, aren't they?

REASON. Yes.

DOUBT. Three different ways of looking at the technology of life, and knowing God is real.

REASON. Yes.

DOUBT. It's hard to argue with your assumed truths.

REASON. Very hard. Unless things are real, and we can use science and our senses to learn about the world, you can't know or prove anything. When only one explanation exists, when you have eliminated the impossible, then that one explanation must be true. If you don't start with my three unprovable truths, nothing in life can be known for certain.

DOUBT. Nothing?

REASON. Nothing. God is real, and we know that as sure as we know anything in this world. Our society is confused and hostile to God. But science tells us God is real.

DOUBT. What do you say to people who think someday science will come up with another explanation?

REASON. I tell them that is not scientific. That is belief in something without facts or logic. It's like saying somebody didn't take your money out of the safe because one day we'll find that money can transport itself to another universe, or that there are invisible money-eating monsters. The only known explanation for technology is that it was designed. God is real.

DOUBT. Amen.

The only known explanation for technology is that it was designed.

The Nonsense of
Cumulative Selection

DOUBT. I'm told there's a problem with your numbers proof. It's called *cumulative selection.*

REASON. Ha! I'm going to enjoy this. Hit me with your best shot.

DOUBT. The first day we talked about life's digital codes—code in DNA and code in the proteins that are built by snapping together amino acids, the building blocks of life. You argued that, since you can't really get working code that does something new by chance, and since every kind of animal has new working code—unique code not related to the code found in any other kind of animal—this proves every kind of animal was designed.

REASON. What a memory!

DOUBT. Thanks, I guess. Anyhow, some say you can easily go from one working DNA/protein code to another working DNA/protein code, even if that code is unrelated, by a process called *cumulative selection.*

REASON. Double ha! That's a common delusion. How?

REASON. Well, as you told me, a working protein is working digital code, a code of linked amino acids created from another code, the code of DNA. Now suppose you start with one working protein/code and there is a mutation, a random change, okay?

REASON. Fine. You have just assumed the existence of life with hundreds of working proteins, which is impossible to get by chance, but okay. Let's *assume* you have a working protein. Accidents happen. Life has technology that copies DNA code very accurately, but once in a while there is a mistake, or the code gets changed in other ways.

DOUBT. Yeah, yeah, whatever. So when a good mutation happens, you keep it, okay?

REASON. What's a good mutation?

DOUBT. A mutation—an accidental mistake in coding—that forms the code to build another working protein, okay? Another protein that life uses.

REASON. Okay.

DOUBT. So you keep hopping from one good mutation to another, and that's how you get new working code, new proteins.

REASON. I see. So one gradual change at a time, one DNA letter changed at a time, is that how it works?

DOUBT. Mostly. But maybe two letters could get changed at the same time or two proteins could get combined.

REASON. So for every working protein, there's another that is closely related? You're right that proteins are linked chains of amino acids. So for every working protein, there's another that just differs in one or two or perhaps even three positions of its amino acid chain, is very closely related to another working protein, or maybe looks like a combination of other working proteins?

DOUBT. Hmmm. Not going to work?

REASON. *No!* Remember orphan genes, what I call *designer genes?* These sections of brand-new working DNA/amino acid coding, that scientists have found in every species, have *no* known relatives. The coding in an orphan/designer gene does *not* resemble the coding in any other gene, and the sequence of amino acids you get from an orphan/designer gene—the new working protein—does *not* resemble any other working protein in any other kind of animal. Each kind of animal contains brand-new unique working coding, both in its DNA and in the special working proteins that are built from that DNA. In the DNA *book* of each kind of animal, there are new paragraphs or even chapters not found in any other book, paragraphs and chapters that don't resemble *any* of the paragraphs and chapters in *any* of the books of *any* other kind of animal.

DOUBT. So designer genes disprove *cumulative selection?*

REASON. Absolutely! The coding in a designer gene does *not* resemble the coding in *any* other gene. Designer genes were *not* created by mistakes in copying other genes. The fifty-four unique codes we have to build parts in our brains don't resemble any other gene. Cumulative selection is rejected by the evidence, by experimental facts. You know what one scientist said was the key to science?

DOUBT. Oh no. You're starting on quotes again. What?

REASON. "If it disagrees with experiment, it's wrong."

If it disagrees with experiment, it's wrong. In that simple sentence is the key to science.
—Richard Feynman, Physicist

DOUBT. So cumulative selection is wrong?

REASON. For sure. Cumulative selection disagrees with experimental facts. There are millions of genes—sections of DNA code—that don't resemble any other gene, and therefore could not possibly have been created by slight errors. Cumulative selection is also mathematical nonsense.

DOUBT. Why?

REASON. You can't get over the probability wall! You can't really create a new, unrelated working gene or protein by chance. The lock is *fantastically* hard to open.

Remember that example of randomly dropping a pin over a piece of paper bigger than the known universe and hitting a dot the size of a carbon atom? That's a probability wall seventy-four feet high, and you have to get over that wall to get a designer gene by chance. When you take a working protein and make random changes, random mutations, it is nonsense to think you are likely to get another unrelated working protein.

DOUBT. But some say you can get any code you want—any working code—by allowing mutations and keeping only the good changes—the ones that get closer to the code you want. Each step is small, and, eventually, you climb over the probability wall.

REASON. Ha! Remember when we compared getting a Shakespeare phrase by chance to opening a bicycle lock?

DOUBT. I do! Sitting down at a keyboard and typing that phrase by chance was like trying to open a bicycle lock with 185 spinning dials and twenty-nine choices on each dial. Even if every atom in the universe was a chicken typing super fast, we couldn't open the lock.

REASON. Brilliant! That's the image. But this *cumulative selection* theory imagines you can easily open that lock!

DOUBT. What? How?

REASON. If you apply the false logic, the false math of cumulative selection, you would say that it's not so hard to get a dial in a correct place by chance, as there are only twenty-nine possibilities on each dial.

DOUBT. Okay, I spin the dials and some may land in the right position, the position they need to be in for the lock to open. Then what?

REASON. According to cumulative selection, you freeze the ones that are right, and spin again the dials that aren't right.

DOUBT. Okay, so I freeze the good ones, the dials that are in the right position to open the lock, and I spin again, and maybe another dial or dials will accidentally fall in the right position.

REASON. Yes. If you keep doing this, you will gradually get more and more right, and, eventually, the lock will open.

DOUBT. I see that. But how do I know which dials to freeze?

REASON. *That's the point!* Cumulative selection is nonsense because it assumes you have a mind in charge of the process, a mind that knows what the end result should be, a mind that *freezes* the dials in the bicycle lock that fall in the right position, freezes the DNA code letters that are correct, until all the dials/DNA letters are exactly right. Cumulative selection requires a mind.

DOUBT. So you can't get over the probability wall by little steps, by *cumulative selection?*

REASON. You're catching on. Darwin's theory has no *search* button. It can't magically find brand-new, unrelated working codes. Science *proves* there is a God.

DOUBT. What do Darwinists say about designer genes, what they call orphan genes?

REASON. Some imagine recipes—take a little code here, a little code there, shuffle them together, reverse this section or that, add a little fairy dust, and bingo, it all works. No one ever explains how you get *over the probability wall!* All of these far-fetched recipes involve a contorted series of steps. They never explain how you get over the probability wall, and why all these unrelated changes could possibly happen, given the fantastic unlikelihood of putting it all together just right.

DOUBT. Darwinists have no explanation for designer/orphan genes, for the brand-new coding in every kind of animal?

REASON. They never say how you get *over the probability wall. Never!*

DOUBT. This is hard to believe.

REASON. Doesn't matter what you *believe!* You loved this quote. "The great thing about science is it's true whether or not you believe in it."

DOUBT. Ha-ha. You and your quotes.

REASON. Cumulative selection is bad math and bad logic.

Doubting Darwin

DOUBT. Talking to you is strange. What I hear, and what I read, is that Charles Darwin completely explained how new species are created, and you don't need God.

REASON. That's the delusion. People are born knowing life is special. But this nonsense that different kinds of animals arose by chance is hammered into you at schools. If you ask questions or disagree, people say you're crazy. Throw in fake science and blatant lies.[11] The result is that most people, even many religious people, are brainwashed and bullied into thinking Darwin's mathematically absurd theory makes sense.

DOUBT. But I hear Darwin's theory explains many things. Some say it explains how animals evolved from a common ancestor.

---

[11] Many are discussed in *Evolution's Blunders, Frauds and Forgeries*, by Jerry Bergman (2017).

REASON. Animals did not *evolve* from a common ancestor.

DOUBT. But I'm told DNA shows connections, relations between different kinds of animals.

REASON. That's what they want you to believe. What they don't tell you is that the connections look different, and the relationships look different, when you look at genes that build different parts of the animal.

DOUBT. So DNA doesn't show connections or relations between different kinds of animals?

REASON. Of course it does. Similar DNA sequences show common *design*. The same designer—God—used similar technology to build different kinds of animals, and that means similar DNA coding and similar genes. But God also put designer genes, new coding, new apps, into every kind of animal. Darwin's theory requires that you get these new designer genes from a chance-based process, and we've seen how that works out. You can't get the designer genes of every animal, the brand-new working codes that make that kind of animal unique, the new codes that are unrelated to the codes for any other kind of animal, the new apps for that animal, from a chance-based process.

DOUBT. How did Darwin say animals were created?

REASON. Darwin published his theory in 1859. Almost a hundred years before DNA was discovered. Nobody knew life runs code.

DOUBT. What did Darwin know?

REASON. He knew living creatures were made up of cells. But he and most people back then thought cells contained only goo. A goo they called *protoplasm.*

DOUBT. Protoplasm? Some sort of goo?

REASON. Yes. They thought cells were a *homogenous blob of protoplasm.*

DOUBT. *Homogenous blob?* What is that?

REASON. A blob with just one kind of goo. All this pretend protoplasm that supposedly did magic stuff.

DOUBT. Just goo? Then how did they explain how life works?

REASON. They didn't. They couldn't! They didn't know life runs code, and they didn't know code builds and runs all the amazing systems that do life's work. Today we know each cell is like a city, with libraries, factories, roads, package delivery systems, storage areas, repair machines, and shredding machines. The simplest cell is far, far more complex than they thought, and has technology more advanced than anything humans have ever created.

> **We tend to think of cells as static, because that's how they were presented to us in textbooks. In fact, the cell is like the most antic, madcap, crowded (yet fantastically efficient) city you can believe.**
> **—Ann Gauger, Molecular Biologist**

DOUBT. Life has advanced technology?

REASON. Technology so advanced it will blow your mind. Fantastic nanotechnology, that works at the atomic level.

DOUBT. No way!

REASON. It's a fact. In 2016, three scientists won a Nobel Prize for finding some of it.

DOUBT. What?

REASON. We have nanotechnology, futuristic and unbelievably tiny machines, in all of our cells. These machines check our DNA and repair it. Different machines fix different types of errors, such as changes in the atoms because of radiation or harmful chemicals. Some machines find broken strands of DNA and snap them back together.

DOUBT. Wow! Darwin didn't know about this technology?

REASON. Bingo! Darwin didn't know cells had any technology, remember? He thought cells were just goo. Life's technology is more advanced than anything humans have ever built.

DOUBT. No way!

REASON. Compare a jet to an eagle. The jet can go faster, but the eagle doesn't need that. It already goes plenty fast to catch food. The eagle is conscious, it can think and it can find its own food. The eagle can do many things the jet can't do, not the least of which is making baby eagles. No machine made by man can reproduce itself from raw materials, yet all living things have this ability.

DOUBT. Wow!

REASON. The Wright brothers studied birds to learn how to fly. Scientists still study the technology of life to learn how God did it, although they don't usually give God the credit.

DOUBT. Scientists study the technology of life?

REASON. You bet. A recent discovery found ways to color clothes without polluting the environment.

DOUBT. How?

REASON. Ever see a peacock?

DOUBT. Yes! Love the colors!

REASON. Those brilliant, iridescent colors don't come from dyes. They are produced by super small geometric structures of atoms, designed to intensify certain wavelengths of light. To design those structures, and build the factories to produce and assemble them, is stunning, futuristic technology. Peacocks didn't get those colors and that technology by accident! But Darwin's theory was not about technology.

DOUBT. It had to do with life getting gradually more complex, didn't it?

REASON. You're not as dumb as you look.

DOUBT. I doubt that's a compliment.

REASON. You got the general idea. Darwin noticed that individual members of a kind of animal can be different. He suggested that if a creature is different in a way that helps that creature to survive, that creature is more likely to bear offspring different in the same way that survive, and so on until this helpful feature or trait gradually, very slowly, spreads through all animals of that kind. This process is called *natural selection.* Darwin's idea was that mutations would create differences, and nature, through natural selection—the survival of the fittest—would gradually select the features or traits each kind of animal needs. Darwin tried to explain all new species by this process of mutation and selection, of picking the best mistakes.

DOUBT. This mutation and then selection process is called survival of the fittest?

Mutations destroy information, they don't create it.

REASON. Yes.

DOUBT. How do you know which animals are most fit?

REASON. The ones that survive.

DOUBT. Wait. The theory is that the animals that survive are the animals most likely to survive?

REASON. Yes. There is no way to determine fitness other than which animals survive.

DOUBT. That's not much of a theory.

REASON. Tell me about it. But it is used to deny God.

DOUBT. Go back to Darwin's idea that small changes can eventually create new kinds of animals. You're saying that reasoning is false?

REASON. It's mathematically absurd to think natural selection can create new technology, new apps, build a different kind of animal. The odds against that are *fantastic*. The probability walls are too high. In the real world, it's impossible to get by chance even one piece of new technology, let alone instructions for building all the pieces, putting them together just right, and running the new technology. But natural selection, survival of the fittest, this process of mutation and selection, can gradually, slowly, make some changes.

DOUBT. Like what?

REASON. Here's a favorite of people who believe Darwin. During the industrial revolution in England there was a lot of pollution, and dark moths became more common.

DOUBT. So?

REASON. When the pollution was cleaned up, white moths became more common.

DOUBT. So?

REASON. A Darwinist would say the birds ate more of the moths that didn't blend in. When the trees were dark with pollution, the birds ate more white moths and black moths became more common. When the pollution was cleaned up, the black moths stood out more, the birds ate more black moths, and the white moths again became more common.

DOUBT. But there were always both black moths and white moths, true?

REASON. True.

DOUBT. Then there was no new technology, and no new kinds of animals. Before the changes there were both black moths and white moths, and all through and after the changes there were both black moths and white moths.

REASON. Yes.

DOUBT. So it was just a temporary change in whether there were more black moths or white moths. No moth changed because of natural selection, and natural selection didn't create any new type of moth, right?

REASON. Yes.

DOUBT. That doesn't show how you get new species. That's supposed to be an example of how evolution can create new species?

REASON. Yes.

DOUBT. That's pathetic. Give me another example.

REASON. Here's another favorite of people who believe Darwin. In the Galapagos Islands off the Pacific Coast of South America, there are birds called finches that eat seeds.[12]

DOUBT. So?

REASON. When there was a drought, smaller seeds became hard to get, but there were still large seeds. More of the finches with larger beaks survived. They could crack open the bigger seeds.

DOUBT. That sounds like a change. Was it permanent?

REASON. No. When the rains returned, the average size of the beaks of the finches went back to normal.

---

[12] Finches are smallish birds found in most parts of the world. According to evolutionary myth, Charles Darwin noticed differences in the size of the beaks of species of finches when he visited the Galapagos Islands in 1835. He supposedly concluded that the birds had adapted, by natural selection, to different diets. Then, a mere twenty-four years later, in 1859, he was inspired by the beaks of finches to conceive and publish his theory of evolution.

Horse manure. As historian of science Frank Sulloway states, "Nothing could be further from the truth." Darwin never mentioned finches in his 1859 book, *On the Origin of Species by Means of Natural Selection, or the Preservation of Favoured Races in the Struggle for Life* (yes, Darwin was a blatant racist). Sulloway writes: "Thus the point of real historical interest is why Darwin, who surely wanted to bolster the text of the Origin with his most convincing scientific evidence, chose to omit any specific reference to a group of birds that he supposedly thought were so important for his evolutionary argument."

History tells us the finch myth, the myth that Darwin had a *eureka* moment while studying the beaks of finches, was made up.

DOUBT. So there were always finches with small beaks and finches with large beaks, this was just a temporary change in the average size of the beak?

REASON. You got it.

DOUBT. That's not new technology! That's as bad as the moth example! Those are silly examples.

REASON. Those are the top two examples most often given to support Darwin's theory.

DOUBT. But no new technology! No new kind of animal! Give me an example of new technology created by natural selection.

REASON. No one has *ever* found new technology created by this process of mutation and selection.

DOUBT. How about in the lab?

REASON. Here's an experiment. Since 1988, scientists have watched a common type of bacteria *evolve* in the lab, grown in flasks with nutrients the bacteria eat. The bacteria reproduce more than six times each day, and there have been over 65,000 generations.

DOUBT. Wow! What happened? Did the bacteria turn into a different kind of creature?

REASON. Nope. Still bacteria.

DOUBT. What happened? Tougher, stronger bacteria?

REASON. The opposite. The bacteria turned into couch potatoes—fat bacteria that can't swim. Because of mutations and errors in coding, some of the technology they used to have no longer works. Because the flasks are shaken and the bacteria don't need to swim to get food, the bacteria got fat and more and more couldn't swim.

DOUBT. Losing the ability to swim isn't new technology! You're saying there was no new technology, no new apps, is that it? Has there *ever* been a situation where natural selection created new technology, a new app for a kind of animal?

REASON. *No!* That has never been seen.[13] Natural selection will never turn a bacteria into a bug, a fish into a whale, or a monkey into a human being.

DOUBT. But I've read some animals can change themselves to adapt. How does that happen?

REASON. Are you ready for the answer? You might want to sit down.

DOUBT. I can take it.

REASON. Some animals have built-in technology to do that. They are preprogrammed to adapt. That is stunning evidence of God. Some animals can actually rewrite their DNA, their operating code. They have extra technology that allows them to write over their DNA code when needed to survive. That's extremely

---

[13] In many cases, natural selection works to preserve a breakdown in technology that confers, for that particular creature, an advantage. A classic example is sickle-cell anemia. Sickle-cell anemia is a human blood disease that, as a side effect, creates a greater resistance to malaria. The malaria virus doesn't thrive as well where sickle-cell anemia is present, so sickle-cell anemia has spread in parts of the world where malaria is common.

advanced technology—totally impossible to get by chance—that proves design.

DOUBT. So natural selection—this mutation/selection process, mutations plus survival of the fittest—can't stumble onto new technology, especially this ability to rewrite code, by chance, is that what you're saying?

REASON. Yes. Natural selection can't invent new apps. Natural selection can only preserve features and traits that already exist. Natural selection doesn't explain how you get totally new working code and totally new technology. Evolution can't find the unbelievably rare codes that build new kinds of animals. There is no *search* button.

Darwin's mechanism of mutation and survival has no search button. It can't find the unbelievably rare codes that build new kinds of animals.

DOUBT. It can't stumble onto the right codes by chance?

REASON. Not really, that's mathematically absurd. As we saw, the odds of getting any sort of new unrelated working protein by chance are *fantastic*. There haven't been enough organisms since the beginning of life to think you would ever get even one new working protein, one *piece* of new technology by chance, much less a bunch of pieces and then assemble and operate them perfectly. The probability walls are too high, the opportunity ladders are too low. Yet scientists have found every kind of animal has designer genes, unique DNA/protein coding that makes that kind of animal different.

DOUBT. Did Darwin invent natural selection?

REASON. People knew about natural selection before Darwin. Darwin went further. Darwin claimed all species are created by completely random mutations and natural selection. That claim is called Darwin's Theory of Evolution. It's a theory of change over time, of evolution without a designer.

DOUBT. But when Darwin suggested it, no one knew life runs code, is that what you're saying?

REASON. Yes. A hundred years later, when DNA code was discovered, many scientists were quick to suggest mutations were caused by changes in the code, and natural selection worked by preserving good sections of code.

DOUBT. Sounds reasonable.

REASON. Not really. If you have working code and deliberately mess it up, insert errors, how likely is it you'll end up with something that makes sense? Take language. If you randomly mess up the letters or spaces, even just a little bit, is it likely to make sense and to say something new?

DOUBT. Maybe not.

REASON. If you take an article or a book and add typos, is it going to get better?

DOUBT. Of course not!

REASON. Suppose you start with a cute little red wagon, like a child plays with, and the complete instructions for building that wagon. These instructions are very detailed, because they tell you how to build each part of the wagon from raw materials and the exact steps to put the wagon together. Then suppose you copy those instructions and make random errors.

DOUBT. Not likely to improve the wagon, is that your point?

REASON. That's part of it. Suppose you do this *lots* of times. Each time you make a few copies with errors, and have a judge who selects the best results, and then you throw away the wagons you started with.

DOUBT. In Darwin's theory, natural selection is that judge, right? And death is like throwing away the first wagon, or the wagons you started with at the beginning of that cycle, that generation?

REASON. Very good! Yes, natural selection, our judge here, picks out the best results of all those mutations. But we lose the first wagon, then we lose the first generation of mutated wagons, and so on, with more errors in the code each generation. We keep doing this, mutating and selecting.

DOUBT. I'm not sure the wagon is going to get better.

REASON. Exactly! Darwin's theory is basically that, if you keep doing this, you will eventually get a space-ship with nuclear technology. His theory—*goo-to-you* evolution—is that life went from a one-celled creature to human beings, with our trillions of interconnected cells and fantastic technology/apps, including the human brain, by this process.

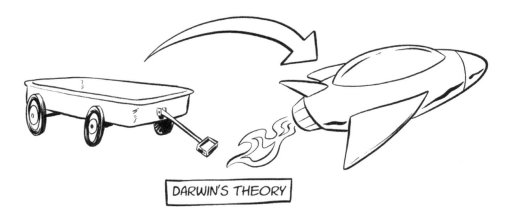

DARWIN'S THEORY

DOUBT. That doesn't make sense.

REASON. Tell me about it! But that's Darwin's theory. If you work through the math on this, you find that not only do you *not* get a spaceship, or any other new technology, but actually, eventually, you no longer have a working wagon. At some point, depending on the mutation rate, the number of errors in copying, the original instructions are so messed up you don't have a wagon.

WHAT REALLY HAPPENS

DOUBT. In other words, mutations destroy information, they don't create it?

REASON. Well said! The facts have never agreed with Darwin's theory. But now we have undeniable proof it is wrong, and that proof is the discovery of designer genes, of new working code in every kind of animal.

DOUBT. Yes. Brand-new code not related to any other code in any other kind of animal, right?

REASON. You got it. In smartphone language, each kind of animal has new apps, new code. Can I go back to the little red wagon?

DOUBT. Sure. Cute example.

REASON. Thanks. Forget the spaceship of human beings. Let's just look at what's needed to turn our little red wagon into something sort of similar. Say a blue tricycle.

CAN THIS HAPPEN BY CHANCE?

DOUBT. Okay.

REASON. To get from a red wagon to a blue tricycle, you need a lot of changes. You need to *evolve* from four wheels to three, with the front wheel larger. You need to *evolve* a seat to sit on. You need to *evolve* handlebars. You need to *evolve* from a wagon frame to a tricycle frame. You need to *evolve* from red to blue.

DOUBT. Got it. Lots of changes.

REASON. Imagine those mutated wagons are rolling off the assembly line. Our judge—natural selection—gets only one choice. It either rejects the wagon—the wagon *dies*—or it keeps the wagon—the wagon *lives* and its code is used to create another generation of wagons. Life or death, that's it. The judge has no control over which errors are made in the coding of the wagons.

DOUBT. Got it. For each wagon, each mutation, natural selection chooses only life or death.

REASON. That's the point! Natural selection can't say, "Well, it sure would be nice to have a seat to sit on, so I'm only going to keep wagons, and let them live, if they start having changes that someday might create a seat." And, really bad for Darwin, natural selection can't simultaneously try to get it all to happen—to *evolve* from four wheels to three, to *evolve* a larger front wheel, to *evolve* handlebars, to *evolve* a tricycle frame, and to *evolve* from red to blue, all at the same time. The facts have never agreed with Darwin's theory.

DOUBT. You say the facts have never agreed with Darwin's theory. That's not what I hear. I'm told *everyone* agrees Darwin's theory of evolution is a fact.

REASON. Blatantly false. Go to dissentfromdarwin.org.

We are skeptical of claims for the ability of random mutation and natural selection to account for the complexity of life. Careful examination of the evidence for Darwinian theory should be encouraged. —Over 1,000 PhD scientists agree with this statement, and they are listed at dissentfromdarwin.org

DOUBT. What's there?

REASON. A list of over 1,000 PhD scientists who don't agree with Darwin's theory. Ever hear of Thomas Nagle?

DOUBT. Don't think so. Is he with the Cowboys?

REASON. No. He's one of the world's top philosophers and a hardcore atheist. Even he and many other atheists strongly doubt Darwin's theory is true. In Nagle's own words, words he used in the title of a book he wrote—Darwin's theory is *almost certainly false.*

DOUBT. Almost certainly false? Alright, so maybe not everyone agrees with Darwin's theory. But you said there are facts. We're not taking a vote on truth. What other scientific facts don't agree with Darwin's theory?

REASON. We could talk for weeks about that, but I'll keep it short.

DOUBT. Good. There's *must see TV* on tonight.

REASON. Well, we already know orphan genes, what I call designer genes, the new, unique working codes in every species, codes that couldn't have arisen from mutations, *prove* Darwin was wrong. Another scientific fact is we've found versions of the same amazing technology in unrelated kinds of animals.

DOUBT. Why would that show Darwin was wrong?

REASON. Because if we find complex, mathematically impossible to get by chance technology in different kinds of animals, kinds of animals that are not closely related, that shows a common designer placed that technology, that app, there for a purpose.

DOUBT. Give me an example.

REASON. Did you know some loggerhead turtles, those large sea turtles that lay their eggs in the sand, migrate across oceans and swim back to lay their eggs years later on the beach they were born?

DOUBT. Maybe.

REASON. Did you know artic terns, small birds, migrate from the North Pole to the South Pole and back?

DOUBT. Maybe not.

REASON. Did you know some salmon swim back from the ocean to the stream where they were born to lay their eggs?

DOUBT. Absolutely! I'm totally on top of that. They climb back up the streams and the bears eat them and—

REASON. Did you know monarch butterflies have a complex migration pattern and return to where their great-grandfathers were born?

DOUBT. What? Seriously? Didn't know that!

REASON. How do you think they all find their way around?

DOUBT. Google maps.

REASON. Ha!

DOUBT. Ask around? Maybe they're not afraid to ask directions.

REASON. Funny. Now get real. How does a loggerhead turtle swim thousands of miles in the open ocean and come back to the same beach?

DOUBT. I give up. How?

REASON. Loggerhead turtles use the Earth's magnetic field.

DOUBT. You mean travel by compass? Pull it out to check every once in a while?

REASON. Funny again. You're right in part. They have compasses built in. And more.

DOUBT. What?

REASON. They can feel the strength of the Earth's magnetic field, not just its direction, and they have built-in code that allows them to adjust for changes, because the Earth's magnetic field keeps changing.

DOUBT. You cannot be serious. You want me to believe a turtle knows the direction and strength of the Earth's magnetic field? You're telling me some turtles use that to find their home beach thousands of miles away?

REASON. These are scientific facts.

DOUBT. I never heard of this. Wow and wow! Seriously? Is that simple technology?

REASON. No, that is advanced technology. To have one, a built-in compass that tells you the direction of the magnetic field; two, the ability to measure the strength of the magnetic field; and three, the programming to use both of them and adapt to changes, requires advanced technology. Humans have been able to do this only recently using computers and sensitive instruments. And here's another fact.

DOUBT. What?

REASON. Loggerhead turtles don't learn this in school. They are *born* knowing how to navigate by the Earth's magnetic field.

DOUBT. I guess all this takes lots of special *parts*, lots of special proteins?

REASON. Of course. *Fantastically* complex proteins put together just right, with incredible operating systems.

DOUBT. And I guess you would argue that, since it is close to mathematically impossible to get a single one of these proteins by a chance-based process involving random mutations, getting all of them, and putting them all together exactly right with processing technology, is never going to happen.

REASON. Exactly! To think this was created by a process involving random mutations is, to quote one scientist, *nonsense of a high order.*

DOUBT. I was hoping you had run out of quotes. And I suppose you would argue that you have to start with all these pieces, that the technology won't work unless you have everything?

REASON. Yes. This system is *irreducibly complex.*[14] You need all the pieces put together just right to make it work.

DOUBT. Did you say this technology is in different kinds of animals?

REASON. Yes! That's crazy unbelievable. Birds have a version of this technology. Some birds can *see*, using technology in their eyes, the direction of the Earth's magnetic field, and, using technology in their beaks, can measure its strength. Similar advanced technology to navigate by the Earth's magnetic field is in some fish, like the salmon the bears eat, some bees, and even some butterflies.[15] These are unrelated creatures.

---

[14] A system is called *irreducibly complex* when, if you take away *any* of the parts, the system doesn't work. The classic example is a mousetrap. If you take away any of the platform, the spring, the hammer, the holding bar, or the catch, the rest of the pieces are useless. Some biological systems, like blood clotting, which depends on a cascade of over two dozen factors to seal a wound, appear to be irreducibly complex. Irreducibly complex systems defy chance-based explanations.

[15] Even some bacteria, lowly single-celled creatures, orient themselves according to magnetic fields. Magnetotactic bacteria are quite common. They manufacture the right size, shape, and kind of material they need, and store it in a compartment that prevents the iron (which is generally toxic to the cell) from damaging other parts of the cell.

DOUBT. Butterflies? Small fluttering bugs have magnetic navigation technology? Butterflies are pretty, even if they are bugs.

REASON. Can I tell you about monarch butterflies?

DOUBT. Go ahead. I still have time before my TV shows start.

REASON. Do you know anything about them?

DOUBT. No.

REASON. Monarch butterflies used to be pretty much everywhere in the United States, but now could be extinct in twenty years. They are gorgeous. Some call them the king of the butterflies.

DOUBT. Is that how they got the name *monarch?*

REASON. I don't know how you figured that out, but yes. Monarch butterflies migrate thousands of miles each year. Some spend the winter in central Mexico, and fly north to the United States or Canada in the summer.

DOUBT. Butterflies? Migrate thousands of miles? With some miniature version of this magnetic navigation system?

REASON. Yes. And there's more. Monarch butterflies totally disprove, shatter, Darwin's theory!

DOUBT. Why?

REASON. No butterfly has ever made the round trip.

DOUBT. What? You just said they migrate thousands of miles to Mexico and back.

REASON. They do, but it takes at least four generations.

DOUBT. What?

REASON. Takes at least four generations. They return to the tree where their great-grandfathers were hatched. Each generation goes from egg to caterpillar to butterfly. The fourth generation, the generation that spends the winter in Mexico, typically lives about six months, and the other three generations live about two months.

DOUBT. They navigate by the Earth's magnetic field, *and* have memory from prior generations? They *know* where their great-grandfathers were born? You cannot be serious.

REASON. I am. These are facts! This technology that allows a butterfly to know, instinctively, where its great-grandfather was born is, well, close to miraculous.

Monarch butterflies navigate by the Earth's magnetic field and return to where their great-grandfathers were born.

DOUBT. I get it. Natural selection couldn't create such a system.

REASON. That's the point! You can't get a migration this complex, with four generations each knowing how to do their part, and with memory from prior generations, by any sort of chance-based gradual process. You either start with all the technology, all the pieces, or you have nothing.

DOUBT. I don't see how a four-generation migration could arise from small, gradual, random changes. I never heard of this. Unbelievable!

REASON. We don't know how this technology works, just like we don't know how the human brain works. Life's technology is more advanced than any technology created by people.

DOUBT. And going back to your navigating by the Earth's magnetic field, how could different versions of that be in unrelated kinds of animals—birds, fish, turtles, butterflies—unless a common designer placed it there for a purpose?

REASON. Sounds like you're beginning to doubt Darwin's theory?

DOUBT. I doubt everything. Doubt is my name. I say prove it, and not only do I see no evidence that anything ever *evolved* from Darwin's mechanism, random mutations and natural selection, but I see many reasons, solid logical, mathematical, and factual reasons, why Darwin's theory is wrong. But what do Darwinists say? How do they explain this technology?

REASON. They say *it evolved.*

DOUBT. Come again?

REASON. They say *it evolved.*

DOUBT. What does that mean?

REASON. Means *it evolved.*

DOUBT. Don't mess. What is the technical, logical, scientific reason that makes thousands of scientists think Darwin's theory of chance-based evolution is true?

Where did the coding to build these systems come from?

REASON. I told you. *It evolved.*

DOUBT. Now you're really messing. They must find a step-by-step pathway that explains how new code came about, right?

REASON. No. They don't. There is no pathway from one designer gene to another. The probability walls are too high.

DOUBT. Then they must find transitional creatures between the two species, right?

REASON. No. They don't. True transitional creatures never existed, except in the imagination of some biologists who believe Darwin.

> **The absence of fossil evidence for intermediary stages between major transitions in organic design, indeed our inability, even in our imagination, to construct functional intermediates in many cases, has been a persistent and nagging problem for gradualistic accounts of evolution.**
> **—Stephen Jay Gould**

DOUBT. Then they must at least do a general mathematical calculation to show how random mutations could have created the new code, right?

REASON. No, they don't. The locks are too hard. The probability walls are too high. No evolutionary biologist *ever* explains how you get over the probability walls.

DOUBT. Do they use a computer to simulate how new species arise?

REASON. No. The computer simulations show mutations lose information, and the arrow of evolution is down, not up.[16]

DOUBT. *Then what do they do?* What's the deal? How can they explain technology this advanced in the head of a butterfly?

---

[16] The most accurate software for simulating the effects of mutation and survival of the fittest over multiple generations is called *Mendel's Accountant.* Mendel's Accountant shows that mutations accumulate in a highly linear manner. Almost all mutations do not have a noticeable effect on fitness, they *sit below* the selection threshold. This results in a continuous increase in the number of mutations in each succeeding generation. It means that all genomes decay over time. Natural selection can only remove the worst mutations, and the majority of mutations, the mutations that are only slightly deleterious, accumulate relentlessly and without limit. These *nearly neutral* deleterious mutations accumulate like rust on a car. Even though an individual spot of rust does not affect the fitness of a car, accumulating rust spots will eventually destroy it. There is no way, for the human race or any other species, to get rid of slightly deleterious mutations.

> **Tom Wolfe was a powerful thinker and writer. His books include *The Electric Cool-Aid Acid Test*, *The Right Stuff*, and *Bonfire of the Vanities* (the last two were adapted into motion pictures). His final book, *The Kingdom of Speech*, points out that Darwin's theory of evolution is not based on science:**
>
> **There are five standard tests for a scientific hypothesis. Has anyone observed the phenomenon—in this case, Evolution—as it occurred and recorded it? Could other scientists replicate it? Could any of them come up with a set of facts that, if true, would contradict the theory (Karl Popper's *falsifiability* tests)? Could scientists make predictions based on it? Did it illuminate hitherto unknown or baffling areas of science? In the case of Evolution... well...no...no...no...no...and no.**
> **(Tom Wolfe, *The Kingdom of Speech* 2016)**

REASON. They can't! There's a monster hole in their reasoning. Whatever we observe, whatever the scientific results are, they just say *"evolution caused it,"* meaning that Darwin's theory of evolution somehow, no matter what the facts are, must still be true.

DOUBT. Be serious. Has anyone ever witnessed new technology created by random mutations?

REASON. I am serious. No one has *ever* seen technology created by random mutations. Mathematically, that can't really happen. But Darwinists have absolute blind faith that random mutations can produce anything, build any technology, turn that little red wagon into a spaceship. This *goo-to-you* theory of evolution is their religion.

DOUBT. Scientists aren't dumb. How could they fall for this?

REASON. Good question. To get a PhD in biology, you almost always have to say you think Darwin's theory is true. If you challenge it, or publicly doubt it, you probably won't get a PhD and, if you do, you probably won't get hired as a professor. They won't let you in the club. If you speak up, you risk being shunned or ostracized, and hundreds of scientists have been fired for exactly that reason.

DOUBT. Scientists have been fired for doubting Darwin?

REASON. Hundreds.

DOUBT. What happened to academic freedom?

REASON. Usually doesn't exist when it comes to Darwin's theory. Not all scientists are Darwinists, but most Darwinists are fanatics. They ignore all facts and viciously attack all challenges. Darwinism is their religion, and they are fanatics.

> **In China, we can criticize Darwin, but not the government. In America, you can criticize the government, but not Darwin.**
> **—Chinese Professor J. Y. Chen**

DOUBT. Well that's sad. People should be allowed to say what they think without being fired.

REASON. Agree. Darwinists have spent their life believing in and defending chance-based evolution, and are too set in their ways to admit this *goo-to-you* stuff is nonsense. Most will never admit defeat. It's up to you, to your generation, to tell the truth.

> **Darwin's theory of evolution is the great white elephant of contemporary thought. It is large, almost completely useless, and the object of superstitious awe.**
> **—David Berlinski**

DOUBT. Wow! And this Darwin delusion has been going on for 150 years?

REASON. Yes. It's the greatest delusion in history; the greatest lie ever presented as *science*. Some say we live in a post-truth world, where facts are not as important as what people want to think. The world is hostile to God. Some people want to deny God, and to do that they have to have absolute, blind faith in Darwin. If you're a biologist and you want to deny that God exists, you have to pretend all technology in living creatures arose from a chance-based process of keeping the best mistakes. You have to be blind to the facts and the probability walls.

> **How cleanly and quickly can the field get over Darwin, and move on?**
> **—Yale computer scientist David Gelernter**

DOUBT. Got it. Let's get back to science. Is there other technology that shows up in unrelated species?

REASON. Lots. Take the appendix.

DOUBT. You can have my appendix. I heard our appendix is useless, which shows human beings weren't designed.

REASON. Darwin himself argued that. Back then people didn't know what the appendix does. It was another argument from ignorance, another argument against God just because we didn't understand how something works. Organ by organ, feature by feature, scientists are discovering items once thought useless are absolutely necessary.

DOUBT. What does the appendix do?

REASON. To begin with, the appendix is a *safe house* for helpful bacteria that may otherwise be destroyed in our stomachs. We now know it serves other critical functions. About fifty species of mammals have an appendix, and those species are so diverse that, to quote one scientist, the appendix "must have evolved separately at least thirty-two times, and perhaps as many as thirty-eight times."

DOUBT. That's amazing, even if you did just sneak in another quote. You're saying this technology arose independently at least thirty-two times?

REASON. At least. These creatures have different versions of the same app. On smartphones, an app can come in different versions. But it's pretty much the same app, designed to do the same thing.

DOUBT. Different kinds of animals have the same basic appendix app, got it.

REASON. So either some blind, undirected, and ultimately chance-based process produced different versions of that app, of the same complex, impossible-to-get-by-chance organ/technology, dozens of times in different kinds of animals, or a common designer placed it there for a reason. What do you think? Either probability walls hundreds of feet high were overcome dozens of times, or the appendix was designed.

DOUBT. Hmmm.

REASON. What do you think?

DOUBT. I doubt Darwin.

REASON. Darwinism is a delusion to deny God. It is contrary to the facts of science, and it is plainly wrong.

Many systems contradict Darwin's theory. Some plants, when attacked, give off signals that tell other plants to create chemicals to discourage attacking animals. It is hard to see how any rational person could claim communication between plants—organisms without brains that don't move—*evolved*. Note the plant being eaten gains no evolutionary advantage by warning other plants.

Origin of Life

DOUBT. I thought science was contrary to God, but your facts about biology and code require a God. Is there other scientific evidence for God?

REASON. Lots! Let's start with something you already noticed. Darwinists believe all life *evolved* from some one-celled organism. But there's an enormous hole in that theory, a hole they will never fill. They will never explain how life could have started without God.

DOUBT. I remember that problem. You said *all* life has digital DNA code and technology to copy and use the code, including futuristic 3-D printers?

REASON. Good memory! You're coming along.

DOUBT. Not thrilled with your *compliments*. So how did life begin? Are you going to tell me it couldn't have begun by chance?

REASON. You *are* starting to get it. The first day we discussed that scientists now know, and this is *the* great discovery in biology in the last century, that life runs code, like computers, only much more complex code. No one has ever suggested a way complex code could arise by chance. But to have life, you need more than code. To have life, you have to be able to reproduce.

DOUBT. So you've got to be able to copy the code?

REASON. That's part of it. You've got to have incredibly lengthy molecules that form a code millions of letters long, and no one knows how that could happen by chance. Then you've got to have molecules that act like machines, such as 3-D printers and copiers that are able to use that exact code. Third, the starting code has to be in the exact right order, so that these machines/molecules can use that code to make copies of themselves.

DOUBT. Slow down. You lost me. So you're saying it's not enough just to start with the code, right?

REASON. Right. A code isn't life. It can't reproduce.

DOUBT. And if I just start with the machines of life, like the 3-D printers or the technology that copies DNA, that doesn't work, either. Is that what you are saying?

REASON. Double right. If you have all the machines but no code, or code that's not in the right order, the machines can't build anything. They can't reproduce themselves. You don't have life.

DOUBT. So to have life you have to start with both the machines and the digital code that those machines can use to build copies of themselves, is that it?

REASON. Triple right! It's an unsolvable chicken and the egg problem. To have life, you have to start with all the machines of life, and a digital code. Even worse, that code has to be in the exact right order so the machines can use it to make copies of themselves.

DOUBT. This is a little hard, but maybe I'm getting it. So I've got to start with a digital code?

REASON. Yes.

DOUBT. And remind me how a digital code can arise without God?

REASON. It can't. Major problem right there.

DOUBT. Okay. But if I've somehow got a code, I've also got to have machines that read and copy the code?

REASON. Yes.

DOUBT. And the starting code has to be in the exact order so the machines of life can use it to build copies of themselves?

REASON. You got it! You have to *start* with everything you mentioned, and actually much more, like machines to collect and use energy, to have life.

Life could not have arisen without God.

DOUBT. You keep talking about these machines of life, but they're not real machines, right, like a toaster?

REASON. Ha ha! No. They are amazing molecules—collections of atoms connected together in particular ways—that perform wonders. The technology of life is more advanced than human technology. When I say life is like a collection of machines, that's a poor description. It's worse than saying the works of Shakespeare are a collection of words.

DOUBT. Shakespeare? That old English dude?

REASON. That's the guy. Some think he was talented.

DOUBT. Don't know him. Has anyone ever figured the odds of getting life by chance?

REASON. Sure. In 1964, a Yale professor calculated the odds of life by chance as one in a number with one hundred billion *zeros*.

DOUBT. Yale? I was going to go there.

REASON. What's wrong with Yale?

DOUBT. Just four letters in the name.

REASON. Of course.

DOUBT. Wait. One hundred billion *zeros*? Do you mean instead the odds are one in one hundred billion?

REASON. No. One in a number with one hundred billion *zeros*. And that's the odds of life ever arising by chance, anywhere in the universe, during the history of the universe, regardless of how many billions of years old you might think the universe is. Ever hear of a *Powerball* or *Mega* lottery?

DOUBT. That's my financial plan. I'm going to win.

REASON. Not smart. You realize the odds of winning could be about one in a billion?

DOUBT. Don't go negative. I'm going *to win!*

REASON. Calm down. You could win. A billion has nine zeros, so winning a Powerball or Mega lottery is like getting over a probability wall nine feet high by chance. Do you think you could win twice in a row?

DOUBT. Hard. I suppose anything's possible, but that's not going to happen.

REASON. Exactly. This professor calculated the odds of life ever arising by chance as less than you winning a Powerball lottery *eleven billion* times in a row.

DOUBT. *Eleven billion* times in a row? That can't happen.

REASON. Exactly. Life couldn't have arisen by chance. The probability wall is *twenty million miles* high. Life forming accidentally is like a tornado ripping through a junkyard and leaving behind a 747 jet, with all systems functional and ready to take off.

DOUBT. Maybe some parts of life happened by chance in one place, and other parts came together in some other place, and so on, and eventually they all hooked up to create life? What about that?

REASON. Pure and absolute fantasy. It all had to happen at the exact same time in the exact same place. Without each other, the complex molecules of life could not survive.

DOUBT. Wait. I remember reading about this in school. There was this *Miller-Urey experiment.* Two scientists showed life could have arisen by chance!

REASON. What did you read?

DOUBT. I remember. These guys tried to copy the atmosphere on the early Earth, and zapped the mixture with electricity, and out popped the pieces of life. Once you have the pieces, anything can happen, you know.

REASON. Nonsense! But you got the general idea right. It was 1963. They produced some of the amino acids that life uses.

DOUBT. Remind me what amino acids are.

REASON. Building blocks of life. Molecules with similar features, including a central carbon atom, that can be snapped together to form chains.

DOUBT. Right, right. The snap-together blocks life uses to build proteins.

REASON. Yes. Proteins are the workhorses of the cell. Our bodies assemble the proteins—

DOUBT. Whatever. Anyhow, these guys zapped some chemicals and ended up with a few amino acids and some other stuff. Doesn't that show life could have arisen by chance?

REASON. Not even close. Even if you start with all the pieces of life, it's ridiculous to think they would get in the right order by chance.

DOUBT. Why?

REASON. The probability wall is too high. Too many choices, not enough time. Remember the odds against getting a phrase with just 185 letters/spaces/exclamation points by chance? Remember how *fantastically* big the number got when we multiplied twenty-nine, the number of choices at each spot, by itself 185 times?

DOUBT. Yeah. Me and all my chickens had no real chance of typing it, even if we typed as fast as theoretically possible for a trillion, trillion years. But my high school textbook really did talk about the Miller-Urey experiment, and suggest life could have arisen by chance.

REASON. It's in a lot of high school textbooks. People who should know better think it explains how life started without God. *It's fake science!*

DOUBT. Whoa! Strong language.

REASON. *Fake science!* Proves nothing! Let me you tell things that *weren't* in your high school textbook!

DOUBT. Sounds like I struck a nerve. Go.

REASON. First, Miller and Urey used the wrong mixture of chemicals.

DOUBT. You sure?

REASON. Here's a quote from Science Magazine in 1995. "The early atmosphere looked nothing like the Miller-Urey simulation."

DOUBT. Okay.

REASON. Second, they only got a few of life's twenty special amino acids.

DOUBT. Okay.

REASON. Third, two main products of the experiment were hydrogen cyanide, which is extremely poisonous, and formaldehyde, which is highly toxic.

DOUBT. Okay.

REASON. Fourth, some of life's chemicals are ridiculously hard to get by any process other than an exact sequence of designed steps.

DOUBT. Okay.

REASON. Fifth, both Miller and Urey later admitted the mere existence of amino acids does not yield life.

DOUBT. That was not in my book. Those guys *themselves* said their experiment does not show life could have arisen by chance?

REASON. Yes.

DOUBT. Then why is this experiment in high school textbooks?

REASON. I'm not done with my list.

DOUBT. What number are we up to?

REASON. Six. The probability wall. You can't get over it, even if you somehow did have all the pieces of life. It's *twenty million miles* high!

DOUBT. Right, no way to get them in the right order by chance. Too many choices, not enough time.

REASON. Ready for my seventh and last reason the Miller-Urey experiment proved nothing?

DOUBT. Yeah, the list is almost over!

REASON. Harvard University launched a massive study to find a way life could have arisen by chance. It crashed and burned.

DOUBT. Harvard? I was going to go there.

REASON. What's with Harvard?

DOUBT. Not highly rated for fun.

REASON. I definitely see how you might find that important.

DOUBT. Of course! What did Harvard try?

REASON. Everything they could think of. In 2006 they launched an *Origins of Life Initiative* and handed out money to people to see if anyone could find a way life could have arisen by chance.

DOUBT. Did it work?

REASON. They held a conference in 2009 with many of the world's top scientists.

DOUBT. And?

REASON. Despite all the money and potential fame being offered, no one could think of a *mildly plausible* way to get life without God.

DOUBT. So what did Harvard do?

REASON. They gave up, but quietly, without admitting only God could create life. Even today's top scientists can't think of a *mildly plausible* way to get life without God.

DOUBT. So maybe your point here is that, if scientists today can't think of a way to get life by chance, to get life without God, Miller and Urey sure didn't come up with one in 1963?

REASON. I don't know how you figured that out, but yes.

DOUBT. Wow! Then why is an experiment that was poorly done and shows nothing in high school textbooks?

REASON. They believe their own propaganda. They choose to be blind to the complexity of life, and how impossible it is to get by chance. Even many college professors are deluded, and they should know better. But if you want to challenge any atheist with true science, just ask how life got started.

DOUBT. What do most say?

REASON. Some say chance, which is worse than ridiculous. But if you can get them to look at the science, to understand the impossibility of getting everything simultaneously by chance, they may just admit they don't know.

> **Imagine 10^{50} blind persons each with a scrambled Rubik's cube, and try to conceive of the chance of them all simultaneously arriving at the solved form. You then have a chance of arriving by random shuffling, of just one of the many biopolymers on which life depends. The notion that not only the biopolymers but the operating program of a living cell could be arrived at by chance in a primordial organic soup here on the Earth is evidently nonsense of a high order.**
> **—Sir Fred Hoyle, Physicist**

DOUBT. But the universe is a big place. Trillions times trillions of stars and maybe more planets. Couldn't life have begun somewhere?

REASON. Not really, and an easy way to see that is to look at the probability wall. The number of planets in the universe may be a number with twenty-five or so zeros. That many chances is an opportunity ladder twenty-five feet high. Now consider all the possible time over the history of the universe and all the possible combinations over that time of all the atoms on all those planets. Estimates differ, but that may extend your probability ladder another hundred feet.

DOUBT. Okay. Am I close?

REASON. Ha! The probability wall is *twenty million miles* high. Those opportunity ladders look silly against that wall. The technology of all life is fantastically complex, and you can't get technology by chance.

DOUBT. That's impossibly high! Some scientists ignore that wall, the probability problem?

REASON. Yes. You sometimes see, not only in newspapers but even in respected scientific journals, an article stating that scientists have found some chemical compound in space that life uses. The article then suggests this may be an important clue in figuring out how life got started. It's absolute, pathetic nonsense, often by people who should know better. Some scientists do this just to get their name in the paper.[17]

DOUBT. Wow! A probability wall *twenty million miles* high? There's no way around this?

REASON. No way. Things can't magically assemble. It takes a mind. Only a mind could create life. That is proof of God.

---

[17] One of the top chemists in the world is James Tour. In January 2019 he gave an excellent lecture on the impossibility of getting life by chance. https://www.youtube.com/watch?v=zU7Lww-sBPg.

> **Life forming accidentally is like a tornado ripping through a junkyard and leaving behind a 747 jet, with all systems functional and ready to take off.**

DOUBT. How can an atheist deny this logic?

REASON. They say "Anything can happen."

DOUBT. I really, really doubt that. What else do atheists do?

REASON. Change the subject.

DOUBT. So science tells us life was designed?

REASON. For sure. Chance is pathetically, ridiculously impossible. We have found something that requires a mind, something that cannot be true without God. Science has found God. True science *proves* God. *No other explanation!*

DOUBT. That is stunning. Are there other areas of science where we see design?

REASON. Absolutely! Another major area is physics—the study of atoms and forces and the laws of the universe. When you take a close look at that, you find the entire universe is designed for life to exist. The universe is perfectly designed for life, and almost all top scientists will admit this is true.

> **"** The more I examine the universe and the details of its architecture, the more evidence I find that the universe in some sense must have known we were coming.
> —Freeman Dyson, Physicist
>
> A common sense interpretation of the facts suggests that a superintellect has monkeyed with the physics, as well as with chemistry and biology, and that there are no blind forces worth speaking about in nature. The numbers one calculates from the facts seem to me so overwhelming as to put this conclusion almost beyond question.
> —Sir Fred Hoyle, Physicist
>
> The laws of science, as we know them at present, contain many fundamental numbers, like the size of the electric charge of the electron and the ratio of the masses of the proton and the electron... The remarkable fact is that the value of these numbers seem to have been very finely tuned to make possible the development of life.
> —Stephen Hawking, Physicist **"**

DOUBT. Then how do they deny design?

REASON. Fantasy. They invent a theory that there are lots of other universes, and invent a theory that the physics of those universes are different, and then say we just got lucky. They deny design by saying "Anything can happen." Utter fantasy.

DOUBT. Other universes? Is that a scientific theory? Can those universes be detected by science?

REASON. Of course not! We can only detect, we can only measure, what's in our universe. This idea of lots of universes, this fantasy they call a *multiverse,* is not the least bit scientific, and it never will be. It can never be tested or disproved. It has absolutely no scientific basis. It's a fantasy to deny the universe was designed.

**The multiverse is not a scientific theory.
It can never be tested or disproved.**

DOUBT. So even though scientists see design everywhere, many deny it?

REASON. Yes. Even people trained in science often choose to ignore facts or to invent explanations that have no basis in true science and can never be tested. This confuses and misleads people. People read articles quoting some scientist saying progress has been made in understanding how life started by chance, and they think it must be true, there must be some truth to the story. People read articles saying this invented concept of a multiverse explains why the universe is perfectly designed for life, and they think the multiverse must be based on scientific fact. But both are *science fiction*.

DOUBT. Can I ask you a question?

REASON. Sure.

DOUBT. If God created the universe, who created God?

REASON. Great question! Science has found that everything that begins to exist has a cause. Science now tells us the universe had a beginning, so it had to have a cause. The Bible tells us God is that cause. God was not created. God just is. That's actually a pretty good translation of what God said to Moses. In the original Hebrew, God's response, when Moses asked for his name, can be translated as "I am existence."

In Exodus 3:13–14, Moses asks the name of God. As translated in the English Standard Version, God responds, *"I Am Who I Am.* And he said, 'Say this to the people of Israel, *I am* has sent me to you.'"

DOUBT. That seems strange.

REASON. It is hard to accept that something can just be, when everything we see had a beginning and was caused by something else. But, logically, you have to start with something that was not caused by something else. Logically, there has to be a *first cause*. According to the Bible, God is that cause. Science has *never* come up with a better explanation.

> **Logically, there has to be a *first cause,* a reason why anything exists. According to the Bible, God is that cause. Atheists have *never* come up with a better explanation.**

DOUBT. This is getting technical, but I read we started with something called a *quantum field,* and that things can pop out of a quantum field, and therefore the universe just popped into existence. Like a *cosmic egg* that somehow *hatched.*

REASON. That's bad science, and does nothing to solve the problem of why anything exists. First, who or what created the quantum field? You are still starting with something that just is. Second, if you say the quantum field just is, has existed forever, then the universe would have popped into existence an infinite time ago, and would have run out of usable energy by now. That is the *Second Law of Thermodynamics.* Third, if matter just *popped out,* then, by the laws of physics, you would have an equal amount of opposite stuff called *antimatter,* and when we look around the universe we don't see antimatter.

DOUBT. That's a little heady, even for a genius like me. What about this idea that you just start with this multiverse thing, an infinite number of universes with different laws and constants of physics, and say that universes can create other universes and so on and so on and Scooby-Dooby-Doo on?

REASON. Funny. Doesn't work. First, who or what caused the multiverse to exist? Second, in the real world, nothing is infinite. Third, there is a scientific theorem that, if there is a multiverse, it can't be infinite, which means, in the words of one scientist: "All the evidence we have says that the universe had a beginning."

> **All the evidence we have says that the universe had a beginning.**
> **—Alexander Villenkin, Cosmologist**

DOUBT. So you've got to start with something that just *is,* that is not caused by or created from anything else?

REASON. Yes. And you don't avoid the proven fine-tuning of the laws and constants of physics, the proven fact that they are perfectly set for life to exist, just by imagining there are other universes with different laws and constants of physics. Just as a bread maker requires more design than a loaf of bread, any mechanism that could create universes with different laws and constants would be more designed, more finely-tuned, than the universes it creates. The multiverse hypothesis just moves fine-tuning out of sight, so to speak. It doesn't eliminate it.

DOUBT. There is no explanation without God for why the universe exists and is designed for life that is based on experimental evidence?

REASON. No explanation based on experimental science.

DOUBT. So belief in a *multiverse,* or some other *first cause* that is not God, has no real science behind it?

REASON. Exactly. There are *science fiction* ideas, but none have a scrap of experimental evidence to support them. There has to be a first cause, something that just exists, and the fine-tuning of the laws and constants of physics is undeniable, even by atheists.

DOUBT. Wow.

REASON. The arrow of modern science points directly to God. When we were less informed, when we didn't fully understand the laws of chemistry and physics, when we were ignorant of the wonders of DNA and the complexity of life, we developed superstitions to deny God, superstitions like Darwinism and the multiverse. But as our knowledge advances, as the technology of life and design of the universe come ever sharper into focus, ever more clear and stunning with each passing year, the old superstitions must go. As the light of science grows brighter, we see God more clearly.

DOUBT. Old superstitions die hard.

REASON. Design is undeniable. God is the only explanation for design in life and design in the universe. Modern science points to God.

DOUBT. To deny God is to deny scientific facts.

REASON. Yes.

DOUBT. Facts like the universe had a beginning and is designed for life.

REASON. Yes.

DOUBT. Facts like the complexity of all life with digital code and molecules that read and copy the code.

REASON. Yes.

DOUBT. Facts like designer genes, new sections of working code in every kind of animal, which prove every kind of animal was designed.

REASON. Yes. You can't get the code of life by chance. You can't get technology by chance.

DOUBT. Facts like the death of Darwin's theory of evolution.

REASON. It's dead. A zombie theory, a theory that has been killed, disproven, in many ways, but people won't admit it's dead.

DOUBT. Disproven by the complexity of DNA with two layers of information and little or no *junk*.

REASON. Yes. Couldn't have arisen from Darwin's mechanism of keeping the best mistakes.

DOUBT. Disproven by the discovery of similar advanced technology in unrelated creatures.

REASON. Yes. Put there by a common designer.

DOUBT. So Darwin's theory is dead.

REASON. Totally dead. Zombie.

DOUBT. And God is the only explanation?

REASON. Yes. Remember your good friend Sherlock. "When you have eliminated the impossible, whatever remains, however improbable, must be the truth."

DOUBT. Ha! But your facts and logic are undeniable. Thank you.

REASON. For what?

DOUBT. The truth.

REASON. You're welcome. Now it's your turn.

DOUBT. To do what?

REASON. Tell others.

" For the wrath of God is revealed from heaven against all ungodliness and unrighteousness of men, who by their unrighteousness suppress the truth. For what can be known about God is plain to them, because God has shown it to them. For his invisible attributes, namely, his eternal power and divine nature, have been clearly perceived, ever since the creation of the world, *in the things that have been made.* So they are without excuse. (Romans 1:18–20, emphasis added) "

GLOSSARY

amino acid. A group of atoms that contains a carboxyl group, with carbon, oxygen, and hydrogen atoms, and an amino group, with nitrogen and hydrogen atoms. Amino acids have a central carbon atom and can be snapped together in chains.

codon. A group of three *letters* of DNA.

Darwinism. The theory that all species arose from keeping the best accidental mutations, and that life was not designed.

DNA. Short for deoxyribonucleic acid, the molecule that contains the genetic code of organisms. The information of DNA is stored in a four-*letter* code.

gene. A section of DNA that contains instructions to build a protein.

multiverse. An invented theory that there are other universes. Since everything we can detect or measure is in our universe, the multiverse theory can never be tested and is not scientific.

protein. A molecule formed by snapping together chains of life's twenty amino acids. A protein is like a machine part of life.

science. Observation, experimentation, and reasoning.

ABOUT THE AUTHOR

Doug Ell brings a unique perspective to the intersection of science and religion. He graduated early from MIT where he double majored in math and physics, and then obtained additional degrees in math and law. A former atheist, he has spent decades studying the evidence for God.

Ell's approach is characterized by wonder and appreciation, rather than dogma. He delights in little-known facts that astonish. His years in logic and law have polished his writing style and give him the ability to explain technical concepts through simple words and pictures.

Ell is listed in *The Best Lawyers in America* and practices law out of Washington D.C.